D1546626

THE PROPHET'S DIPLOMACY

THE PROPHET'S DIPLOMACY

The Art of Negotiation as Conceived and Developed by the Prophet of Islam

by

AFZAL IQBAL

Foreword by S. A. Rahman
Preface by Muhammad Daud Rahbar

CLAUDE STARK & CO.

CAPE COD, MASSACHUSETTS 02670

Library of Congress Cataloging in Publication Data
Iqbal, Afzal.
    The Prophet's diplomacy.

    Earlier ed. published under title: Diplomacy in
Islam.
    Bibliography: p.
    Includes index.
    1. Muhammad, the prophet—Political career.
2. Diplomacy. I. Title.
BP77.69.I65   1975   327'.2'0924   [B]
ISBN 0–89007–006–7   74–20174

PRINTED IN THE UNITED STATES OF AMERICA

TO
MY DAUGHTER
REHANA

لَقَدْ كَانَ لَكُمْ فِى رَسُولِ اللَّهِ أُسْوَةٌ حَسَنَةٌ

Verily in the messenger of Allah ye have a good example. . . .

(The Qur'an, XXXIII, 21)

ACKNOWLEDGMENTS

I owe a debt of gratitude to the late Maulana Abul Kalam Azad for his guidance and help in preparing the plan of this book. I am also grateful to Sir Muhammad Zafrulla Khan, Maulana Abdul Majid Daryabadi and Professor Shahid Suhrawardy for reading the first draft and giving me their valued comments. My thanks are due to Professor Bernard Lewis of the School of Oriental Studies, London, Mr. Bazmi Ansari of the Central Institute of Islamic Research, Karachi, and my old friend Dr. Muhammad Ajmal of the Government College, Lahore, for many useful discussions. I am indebted to Justice S. A. Rahman of the Supreme Court of Pakistan and Professor M. M. Sharif, Director, Institute of Islamic Culture at Lahore, for their constant encouragement. Other helpers have been many, particularly my colleagues in the Pakistan Foreign Service, and to them I offer my heartiest thanks. And finally I avail myself of this opportunity to express my sincere gratitude to my wife for her understanding and provocative criticism which led to many material changes. This book was written during the time which legitimately belonged to her.

CONTENTS

The First Act of Arbitration—Muhammad in Mecca: Persecution *versus* Negotiation—The First Treaty of Islam: Covenant with Medinians and the Jews—The Battle of Badr—The Battle of Uhud—The Treaty of Hudaybiya—Muhammad's Conduct as the Conqueror of Mecca—Conciliating the Ansar at Hunayn—Dealings with the Hypocrites—Slander on 'A'yesha.

I. Delegations Received by the Prophet: Ta'if, Christians of Najran, Banu Sa'd, Banu Tayyi', Banu Tamim, Banu Hanifa, Kings of Himyar, Kinda.

II. Delegations Dispatched by the Prophet: The First Embassy of Islam: Mission to the Negus; Instructions to Envoys; Envoys to Various Kingdoms

3. THE MORAL DIPLOMACY, 82

Gentleness in Human Relations—Trust in Truth—Faithful Communication—Patience for a Cause—Modesty and Moderation—Loyalty

FOREWORD
by S. A. Rahman

In the context of interstate relations the word *diplomacy* seems to have acquired a bad odour.

This is an instance of history projecting itself into semantics. The Machiavellian tradition effected a divorce between the art of negotiation and the moral imperative in the national and international fields. But this tradition carried within itself the seeds of its own nemesis. It has left a trail of bitterness, suspicions and misunderstandings in its wake which continue to bedevil human relations.

Is it possible, then, to conceive of a 'clean diplomacy' without the mean subterfuges, the degrading deceit and the heartless hypocrisy that have come to be associated with the traditional figure of the diplomat? Does history furnish evidence of such diplomacy in action bearing fruitful results? Dr. Afzal Iqbal has addressed himself to these questions in his book and has answered them in the affirmative.

He has found the perfect exemplar in this respect in the person of the Prophet of Islam, Muhammad (on him be peace). The author has undertaken an interesting and instructive study of an aspect of the Prophet's comprehensive career which has received only cursory attention at the hands of his biographers. He has analysed the various situations with which the Prophet was confronted in his lifetime in order to place his approach in its proper perspective, and has shown conclusively that because his strategy in peace and in war was superb in conception and execution it therefore paid the richest dividends in terms of human welfare. At the same time, he deviated not one inch from the high moral plane on which the prophetic consciousness moves and has its being. The ends he had in view and the means he adopted were alike above cavil or criticism. Dr. Afzal Iqbal is himself a member of our diplomatic service, and if his book succeeds in kindling the diplomatic conscience and conditioning its subjective processes for the realisation of the highest human values, his book will have served its purpose.

S. A. RAHMAN
Former Chief Justice
Supreme Court of Pakistan

Lahore, Pakistan
18 June 1961

PREFACE
by Muhammad Daud Rahbar

The teachings of the founders of the world's great religions have a potency which is due to their relevance to
life and their miraculous simplicity. The Prophet's mono-
theism is forthright and uncomplicated. In it there is
a challenge for haughty tyrants and hope for the victims.
Ultimately in it there is hope for all.

Muhammad was distressed by certain conditions in his
time. Highways were not safe to travel. Arab tribal society
was led by hoodlums whose wild and impetuous nature
presented a constant hazard to householders, nomads and
pedestrians. The Prophet dreamed of an integrative, in-
clusive and expanding community sharing beliefs, com-
modious culture and a wide scope of human experience.
He won over the seditious chieftains with challenging but
compelling words. The conversion of many strong men,
particularly the forthright kinsman 'Umar (in the sixth
year of the Prophet's mission) represented eloquent
portents of irreversible change.

Ideally speaking, the community of the faithful, called
the *ummah* by the Muslims, is opposed to tribalism.
Muslims call the pre-Islamic Arabia the country of
ignorance or stupidity (*jahl* or *jāhilīya*). Contextual
study of the Qur'ān's allusions to *jahl* has established that

the Prophet identified it with blind impulsiveness and capriciousness. To him the opposite was a combination of prudence, forbearance, discipline, self-restraint, persuasiveness, compassion and forgiveness. It was not *'ilm* (knowledge) but *ḥilm* (forbearance) which mattered. Most importantly, the foundations of the *ummah* rest on trust and not suspicion. Duplicity runs counter to the spirit of the Prophet, which is characterized by honesty, openness and disdain for secretiveness.

The Amnesty of Mecca (630 A.D.) is the crowning event of Muhammad's career. It was the culmination of his mission whereby the tribal law of unrelenting retaliation was abrogated. In the hearts of all Muslims this amnesty implies the Prophet's will to intercession. By commemorating it the Muslim renews the hope of divine forgiveness, trusting fully that the Prophet will intercede firmly and save the guilty. That is why the eyes of Muslims are moistened by tears at the mention of Muhammad. That is why the Muslims call him the Mercy for the Worlds.

The Prophet believed in persuasion and in education by example. The battlefield was for him the last resort for defending a righteous cause. But when forced into fighting for human rights, he did not flinch. That is one of the manifestations of his straightforwardness. Another is his teachings, which established a religious tradition based on respect for the basic human appetites, desires and aspirations. Although himself capable of great austerity, he did not preach asceticism to others. He never said, "Eat like wolves and drink like fish." Nor did he say, "Be celibates, starve, walk on cinders and kill the ego." Rather his message is "Refresh and fortify both selfhood and community." He did not instruct his listeners to become either revellers or renouncers. In other words, he taught healthy, honest and responsible citizenship.

No wonder Muslims call Islam the religion of naturalness (dīn-i-fiṭrat). The revelation of the Qur'ān, with which the Prophet's personality is fully harmonious, does not put impossible demands on the will of the believers. It reasonably leaves the question of the degree of the individual's renunciation to the individual's capacity. Nevertheless greed and materialism are constantly condemned in the Qur'ān.

Muhammad employed diplomacy as a means of education. The Prophet-King of Arabia is the only king in world history who never lived in a palace, whose seat of power was practically a mud hut, and who had only one piece of furniture in his reception room for envoys: a leather-covered bolster. This he offered to his guests, contenting himself with the solid earth for his own seat.

Those among the Prophet's companions who became his successors, called the Caliphs, were not his spiritual equals. They launched the Islamic mission in a way which was not exactly the Prophet's way, commencing rapid military conquest and rapid conversion of other nations to Islam. History is indeed a mystery. The Caliphal empire was an accomplished fact within two decades after the Prophet's passing away. It included North Africa, the Middle East and Central Asia. The early politics of a huge empire both implemented and transformed Islam.

A major development was some reassertion of tribalism and the emergence of nationalism. The Arab and Iranian interests clashed. The secretive Shī'ite movement, adopted by the Iranians as a vehicle for nationalist activity, introduced some strategic secretiveness (taqīya) in some sections of the Muslim community. It was different from the open-faced statesmanship of Muhammad. However, we have to accept these developments as valid and inevitable compromises that an expansionist religious organization has to go through. Buddhism, Christianity and Islam could not have become world religions without compromises. Compromises represent adaptation and adjustment for survival.

It might be profitable to compare the expansion of Islam with the heritage of the West in relation to its politics, diplomacy and statesmanship. The Prophet became the King of Arabia two years before his death. His immediate successors conquered some twenty countries within fifteen years. This story is very different from that of the Christians, who underwent four centuries of secret and persecuted existence. With the conversion of Constantine much of Christian life came out into the open, yet the troubled first four centuries may continue to condition the psychology of the Christian community today. Christians now make up almost a third of the world's population; yet they cannot stop identifying themselves as a persecuted minority. This is the force of historical habit. We see a continuing phenomenon in the community of heightened vigilance, secretiveness, alertness, preparedness and exclusiveness. Detective drama and detective fiction are the most popular means of public entertainment.

The modern West has much to learn from the unsophistication of Islamic diplomacy. For if that does not happen, the non-Westerner will learn from the West the methods of secretive strategy. This will turn the world more and more into a jungle of misused intelligence: intrigue, espionage, ambush, mistrust and an unbreaking cycle of retaliation. Unprophetic, selfish, shortsighted, short-range diplomacy is destined to meet with failure.

World history following the World Wars has taught this lesson. The Qur'ān illustrates the point:

> They were clever, but God was clever too, for God is the best of clever ones. (8:30)

The cocktail-party approach to diplomacy, with its suave talk and confounding tactics, will not benefit any nation in the coming decades. Solemn concern for international cooperative planning, coordination and trust are the only sound principles of redemptive and constructive diplomacy. Ambassador Iqbal has written an inspired book, one which should be read by all diplomats. God reward him for his effort.

Boston, Massachusetts
March 24, 1974

INTRODUCTION TO
THE AMERICAN EDITION

I am happy that the essay on the Prophet's diplomacy which was originally published in Pakistan over a decade ago under the title *Diplomacy in Islam* is now being made available to the American reader. Professor Arnold Toynbee, commending my book *The Culture of Islam* once remarked that the knowledge of Islam, its culture, and its history is minimal in the United States and that this ignorance has had unfortunate effects on American foreign policy.

More than six hundred million Muslims living all over the world have a way of life and a point of view. It is a far cry from the days when Turkey was the only Muslim state which was admitted into the League of Nations. In February 1974, nearly forty Muslim states participated in the Islamic Summit in Lahore. The Arabs who were dismissed not long ago as Bedouins have now come to acquire a say in the affairs of the contemporary world. It is of the utmost importance, therefore, to understand a segment of society which has long been ignored and in fact frowned upon. Their past has not been very pleasing to some, but their future, however dark it may seem to those who are blinded by prejudice, is pregnant with untold possibilities. One thing is clear. The spirit of the

Crusades which has long pervaded the West is now ir-
relevant and counterproductive. The Muslim world is
not on a collision course. It seeks cooperation and understanding on a basis of equality. It is high time that the
common heritage of Christianity and Islam received the
recognition it so richly deserves.

It is a sign of the times that an American publishing
house should seek to disseminate the Muslim view of
diplomacy to its readers. In a world torn by endless
violence the art of negotiations has a contribution to
make to the cause of peace. The Muslim concept of
diplomacy, as conceived and practised by the Prophet of
Islam, should be meaningful not only to Muslims but to
others who have to deal with them. If this essay can help
enlarge the area of goodwill and understanding even by
the fraction of an inch, my effort will have been amply
rewarded.

AFZAL IQBAL

Stockholm
March 23, 1974

INTRODUCTION
TO THE SECOND EDITION

It is a matter of deep satisfaction to me that the essay on diplomacy in Islam has been widely welcomed in the Muslim world. The quick disposal of the first edition is indicative of the measure of appreciation so generously given by the reader. I am grateful to many scholars who have offered valuable suggestions most of which I have tried to reflect in the revised edition. The essay remains incomplete in that it is no more than an effort at provoking further study in this field. This purpose has, however, partly been served in that the book has been widely distributed among practising diplomatists in the Muslim world but I still look forward to one of our young colleagues producing a more comprehensive work on the subject.

AFZAL IQBAL

New Delhi
1 September 1965

INTRODUCTION
TO THE FIRST EDITION

International law, as we understand its origins today, sought to regulate the conduct of Christian states in their intercourse with each other. This was the position until 1856. Turkey was the first non-Christian state to gain admission into the comity of nations, but her position remained anomalous until 1923. The West considered her inferior in civilisation and would not treat her on an equal footing. Modern international law is in fact the law which originated in Western Europe. It is not surprising, therefore, that in dealing with its history, all the standard works on international law and diplomacy begin with the Greek city-state, describe the Roman period immediately following, and then suddenly jump to modern times, ignoring a period of no less than a thousand years which intervenes, asserting that during the Middle Ages 'there was no room and no need for an International Law.'[1]

This period which is dismissed as the dark age of diplomacy saw the birth and growth of Islam. Rising from Mecca it flashed into Syria; traversed the whole breadth of Northern Africa; and then, leaping the straits of Gibraltar, it hammered at the doors of Europe. Islam achieved its full political maturity within the first century and its greatest geographical extent during the first seven hundred years of its existence. It conquered Sicily and reached as far as the Campagna and Abruzzi in the south of Europe. Using Spain as a springboard it jumped into Provence, Northern Italy, and even to Switzerland. From its stronghold in Spain and Sicily it transmitted its powerful cultural influences to the whole of Europe. Baghdad in the East and Cordova in the West were the greatest centres of learning in the Middle Ages. This was the period which saw the beginnings of the European civilisation. The earlier European writers on international law, such as Pierre Bello, Ayala, Vittoria, Gentiles and others, hailed from Spain or Italy, and owed much to the renaissance provoked by the impact of Islam. Grotius, father of European international law, and other early writers we have mentioned drew heavily on Arabic works. It is difficult to trace their sources to Greek and Roman works. In fact they provided the missing link between the Roman and the modern period and serve to give a clue to the far-reaching changes brought about by Islam in the concept of international law.

The Hebrews evolved a culture of their own under Moses and the Divine Pentateuch. The Jews refused to recognise other groups. They were sworn enemies of some foreign nations such as the Amalekites with whom they refused to have any relations in war or in peace. The Greeks looked upon all non-Greeks as barbarians. Aristotle believed that 'nature intended barbarians to be slaves.'[2] In any case the Greeks did not have a powerful national state before the conquest of Macedonia. The Romans conquered the Greeks, but the political conquest did not bring about any radical change relevant to international law. In fact, Greece reconquered Rome intellectually. Oppenheim has no difficulty in conceding that the influence of Christian teaching was not visible although Christianity became the state religion under Constantine the Great (c.e. 306–37). When the Roman Empire was divided, all the people belonging to the eastern wing were considered barbarians although they had adopted Christianity. The life and property of the citizens of a state which had no treaty of friendship with Rome was not safe in Roman territory. Such people had no rights, their property could be seized and they could be made slaves.[3]

With the emergence of Islam we see the establishment of a principle which was to prove revolutionary for international law and diplomacy. Islam proclaims the equality of man:

> O mankind! Lo! We have created you from a single male and female, and We have made you nations and tribes that you may distinguish one from another. Lo! the noblest of you, in the sight of God, is the one who feareth (Him) most.[4]

The distinction between Greeks and barbarians, Jews and Amalekites, Romans and the inferior Eastern Christians is abolished. Prejudices based on colour, race and language are condemned. All states, all men, irrespective of religion or race, are proclaimed as possessing similar rights and obligations:

> Lo! those who believe (in that which is revealed unto thee, Muhammad), and those who are Jews, and Christians, and Sabeans—whoever believeth in Allah and the Last Day and doeth right—surely their reward is with their Lord, and there shall no fear come upon them, neither shall they grieve.[5]

Islam provides for the first time the idea of a universal state based on the equality of man. In Muslim law for the first time, we come across rights for the enemy in all times, in peace as much as in war, rights endorsed by the Qur'an and the Prophet. The international law of Islam seeks to regulate the conduct of a Muslim state on the justest possible basis, not only with other Muslim states but with the whole non-Muslim world. Grotius, father of European international law, mentions on the occasion of compiling his book[6] that in his time the Christian nations of Europe behaved in their wars in a manner of which even barbarians would be ashamed. Early books on *jura belli* (laws of war) by European writers are indeed echoes of Arabic works on *Jihad*—and here we see the role played by Islam in the history of international law.[7]

This role is not even mentioned, much less recognised, by the Western authorities on international law and diplomacy. While they find no difficulty in conceding the influences of Jewish and Christian civilisations they dismiss the whole chapter of Islam as a dark age. This is inconsistent with the scientific spirit. After a long struggle Christianity has learned to coexist with Islam. Indeed Islam may be increasingly recognised as being a bridge between the warring ideologies of the East and the West. One would therefore expect greater understanding and sympathy from the West, which has unfortunately read and taught biased accounts of Islam over the centuries.

What is more serious, however, is the fact that the Muslim student, ill-equipped to go to the original sources, tends to accept the version of his own history and traditions from foreign sources. He is essentially a product of European education and cannot help assimilating the subtle influences which seek to undermine the basis of his own culture. The modern Muslim intellectual, reared in the Western traditions of thought and feeling, tends to lose sight of his own intellectual and cultural heritage. The Western tradition of inquiry, exploration, research and analysis is a valuable instrument, but the Muslim intelligentsia in our countries appear incapable of employing this instrument for an understanding of their own past. However humble one's past may be, it is a fount from which direction for the future can flow. Our past is spiritually and materially rich and varied. In fact it contains the germs of rational thought and instruments of research sharpened and made more refined by scientific research. It was Muslim philosophers and thinkers who for the first time successfully challenged Aristotelian logic and demonstrated that this logic was inadequate to meet the growing demands of scientific knowledge. Muslim thinkers like Ibn Taymiya showed that a syllogism was really tautologous, and that consequently it could not embody new knowledge. We can therefore adopt the Western instruments of research without a feeling of estrangement and use them to discover our own past.

We in fact live in isolation from our own people. Our feet are in the Orient but our minds move with the currents emanating from Cambridge, Oxford, Cornell and Harvard. This state of emotional dissociation with our people creates in us a dread of being engulfed in our problems if we should dare to face them. But it is precisely an inquiry into our past and the problems arising therefrom which can sustain us in the present and determine our fate in the future. Whether we like it or not, we will have to look at our tradition anew in a concerned way, and not with the impersonal objectivity of the Western historian.

International law today is no longer a law between Christian states only. With the emergence of a large number of Muslim states, it has become necessary, even for the non-Muslim states, to pay increasing attention to an understanding of Islam and all that it stands for. The sources of Islamic law of nations belong to the well-known categories defined by modern jurists, viz. agreement, custom, reason and authority. The Qur'an provides the authority, the *Sunnah* (practice and precept of the Prophet) represents the custom, the rules stated in treaties fall under the category of agreement, and the opinions of caliphs and subsequent jurists belong to the category of reason. In this monograph an attempt has been made at a study of the first two sources, i.e. the Qur'an and the *Sunnah* of the Prophet. While some work has been done in the sphere of international law by a few Muslim scholars, the field of Muslim diplomacy has not received the attention it deserves.

What is diplomacy? What is the diplomacy of Islam? What is the concept of diplomacy which emerges from the Qur'an and the practice of the Prophet? Or is the word *diplomacy* too unwholesome to be associated with the Prophet? These are some of the questions that need to be answered.

'Diplomacy' is a much maligned expression. It has been used to denote many shades of meaning most of which are incompatible with honest virtue, let alone the standards set by a prophet. Even the ordinary diplomat feels embarrassed today that Hermes should have been selected as a tutelar deity of his profession. The first associations of charm, trickery, cunning, flattery and deception springing from Greek origins have continued to be associated with diplomacy in varying degrees. Diplomacy did not completely shed its vicious traits under the Romans nor did it succeed in acquiring a moral basis. It was a British ambassador, Sir Henry Wotton, who in a moment of cynicism expressed the view that 'an ambassador is one who lies when abroad for the good of his country.' The phrase[8] cost him his job, but it has stuck in the popular imagination which continues to associate diplomacy with traits of character which may not bear any relevance to functions of modern diplomacy. From being merely the business of dealing with archives or 'diplomas,' as the Greeks called them, diplomacy has developed into an elaborate science dealing with international affairs. The word *diplomacy,* as applied to the conduct of international affairs, did not become current in the modern sense until 1796, when Edmund Burke used it in this context. The Oxford dictionary provides the following definition, which will help in an understanding of the issues involved:

> Diplomacy is the management of international relations by negotiation, the method by which relations are adjusted and managed by ambassadors and envoys: the business or art of the diplomatist.

A diplomat, then, is a negotiator *par excellence.* Diplomacy as the art of negotiation existed before Islam. In Greek mythology, Hermes, the god of diplomacy, is credited with charm, deception and cunning—the subtle arts with which he endowed Pandora, the first woman who wrought havoc with her gifts of flattery and deceit. In the Homeric period the main qualifications for diplomacy, conducted by the early herald, were a retentive memory and a loud voice. The consummate ingenuity of the Byzantine emperors in conducting negotiations by coercion and corruption is all too well known. The unwholesome record of the Papal Chanceries of the medieval period as also the conduct of those who were responsible for the disrepute that diplomacy inherited from the Middle Ages need not be dealt with here, nor need we discuss the role played by the Florentine diplomats of the Renaissance like Dante, Petrarch, Boccaccio and their later pupils like Guicciardini and Machiavelli.

In the context of the antecedents of modern diplomacy a study of an outline of diplomacy in early Islam is rewarding. Some of the main objectives of diplomacy being a peaceful solution of international problems and promotion of harmony between different states, it should be of interest to see how the Prophet, who was also the head of a state, achieved these objectives by the well-known methods of diplomacy, i.e. negotiation, conciliation, mediation and arbitration. There are extant a large number of biographies of the Prophet, but no significant attempt has so far been made to analyse his life as a negotiator. And yet from a study of the Qur'an and the life of the Prophet a picture does indeed emerge of the fundamentals of diplomacy in Islam. How far the fundamentals were followed by his successors is a question which does not fall within the purview of this monograph, which confines itself to a study of the Prophet's life with a view to understanding the character and qualities of diplomacy in Islam.

This essay is a dialogue on two levels. It is a dialogue with the European historian who has ignored the role of Islam while recording the history of diplomacy, thus leaving a serious intellectual gap which cannot be filled by labelling an important period of history as 'dark middle ages.' This essay is also an inner dialogue. Its purpose is to enter into conversation with the followers of Islam. Since in all things, great and small, the moral sanction and inspiration for a Muslim is the teaching of the Qur'an and the life of the Apostle, a Muslim diplomat must relate his religious orientation to his profession. This relationship has to be consciously realised to avoid a dissociation of personality. No one can legitimately hold that life can be divided into religious and moral aspects on the one hand and the professional on the other. Both these aspects imply each other. Islam has above all emphasised the unity of personality because without this unity there can be no wholeness or sincerity.

This essay is a modest beginning. It opens up further avenues of research and exploration. A great deal can be done and achieved if our young diplomats with a scholarly turn of mind devote a part of their energy to relating the needs of their profession to their cultural and religious heritage. My purpose will be amply served if a further probe is attempted in this rich and largely ignored area of thought and culture.

For historical data used in this book I have depended upon Ibn Ishaq's *Sirat Rasul Allah*. It has recently been translated by Alfred Guillaume into English (*The Life of Muhammad*, London, Oxford University Press, 1965). I have also used the voluminous work in Urdu by Shibli and his able successor, Sayyid Sulayman Nadvi. For translations of the Qur'an, I have consulted the explanatory but incomplete translation by the late Maulana Abul Kalam Azad; almost all English extracts reproduced in the text have been taken from Marmaduke Pickthall's translation, *The Meaning of the Glorious Koran*. I have preferred the current *diplomat* to the correct *diplomatist* which sounds somewhat pompous.

Afzal Iqbal

Bangkok
1 August 1961

CHAPTER

1

PRINCIPAL NEGOTIATIONS

THE FIRST ACT OF ARBITRATION

The first glimpse that we get of the diplomat in Muhammad comes long before he was invested with the role of prophethood. The scene is Mecca. Muhammad is in his twenties. A dispute arises out of the reconstruction of the Ka'ba—the most important place of worship inherited by the Quraysh from Abraham. All the tribes of Mecca join hands in raising a new building. The Ka'ba must have the best material. Timber is purchased at the port of Jeddah and a Roman is engaged as an adviser. The labour of love continues smoothly till the work is almost complete. Only the Black Stone—the stone of destiny—remains to be fixed. But who is to do this? All the tribes which have worked so hard to complete the building claim the final honour. The tribes which worked together with a singular devotion now go their several ways, form alliances, and get ready to fight. One[1] brings a bowl full of blood; another[2] joins in and the bloodlickers (as they were called) pledge themselves unto death and thrust their hands into blood—a ceremony which symbolises their determination to offer the supreme sacrifice—indeed a most critical situation. Tension is high and what makes it dangerous is that it has continued for four days. At last on the fifth it is agreed, at the suggestion of the oldest living Qurayshite,[3] to accept as arbitrator the first man who enters the temple the next morning. This is not a decision but an evasion; it only helps to intensify the terrible drama of the situation which is pregnant with dangerous possibilities. Hot-headed Arab chiefs wait with breathless anxiety. Their feelings of expectancy have been roused to the highest pitch. The future is unpredictable and there is a whole night between them and the final award. With nerves taut and in alternating waves of hope and fear, the long hours of the dark night seem to stretch into infinity. With the dawn of the day they see young Muhammad enter the temple.

When they see him they say: 'This is the trustworthy one. We are satisfied. This is Muhammad!' Here, then, is the arbitrator that all the important leaders of Mecca have awaited in eager expectation for a whole night. It now falls on his young shoulders to bear the burden of a decision which has baffled the Arab chiefs for the best part of a week. This is a challenge indeed to his capacity for tact and judgment, for the slightest error would throw the whole of Mecca into a bloody conflict. No diplomat in Muhammad's position would have envied the assignment given him without warning. And yet if the situation is to be saved, a decision has to be negotiated. There is no time for vacillation and delay. The nerves of the contesting parties are taut; and an award which fails to satisfy the claims of all concerned is bound to lead to strife and worse. But Muhammad shows no signs of nervousness. He is not daunted by the magnitude of the task. He proceeds to pronounce his decision as an arbitrator—a decision which at once satisfies the claims of all the contesting parties and averts the bloodshed which had appeared imminent only a few moments before his arrival on the scene. He asks for a sheet of cloth. When it is brought to him he takes the Black Stone, puts it inside and asks each tribe to hold an end of the cloth and lift it together. This decision associates all the leaders of the tribes with the act of carrying the Black Stone to its proper place in the wall of the Ka'ba. Muhammad asks each of the contesting tribes to select a representative. He then spreads out the cloth to the level of the wall where the stone has to be fixed. They all thus share the honour for which they were threatening to kill each other! And he saves the situation by himself taking up the stone and fixing it in the wall without the slightest protest from any side—in fact in the midst of grateful acclaim from all directions.

Thus the highest qualities of tact and judgment save a situation which seemed impossible to settle otherwise. This was the first time in Muhammad's life that these qualities found public expression and won instant recognition. Muhammad at this time was not a prophet and was less than twenty-five years of age.[4]

MUHAMMAD IN MECCA: PERSECUTION VERSUS NEGOTIATION

The Quraysh, who acclaimed Muhammad as the 'trustworthy one' and hailed him as a great arbitrator who had wisely averted bloodshed in Mecca, were soon to turn against him.

Muhammad was forty years of age when he received his first revelation. Three more years were to elapse before he published his faith. The first meeting he convened consisted of forty men of the Quraysh. When the Apostle wanted to address them, Abu Lahab, his uncle, got in first and said, 'Your host has bewitched you,' so they dispersed before Muhammad could address them. The next day he asked them to a meal and made his first speech as a prophet. 'O sons of 'Abd Muttalib,' he said, 'I know of no Arab who has come to his people with a nobler message than mine. I have brought you the best of this world and the next. God has ordered me to call you to Him. So which of you will cooperate with me in this matter?'' The men remained silent. 'Ali who was the youngest, most rheumy-eyed, and thinnest in legs was the only one to respond. He was a mere lad of ten. Nobody took him seriously. The old men got up laughing and jeering.

The mission could not be abandoned simply because the wise men of the Quraysh had failed to respond. Muhammad took the message to the mass of the people; he stood in the vale and said, 'O sons of 'Abd Muttalib; O sons of 'Abd Munaf; O sons of Qusayy'—he named the Quraysh tribe by tribe until he came to the end of them and said: 'I call you to God and I warn you of His punishment.' The response was lukewarm. The people did not withdraw or turn against him until he spoke against their many gods. When he did, they took great offence and resolved to treat him as an enemy. He was, however, safe in the protection of his uncle Abu Talib and continued to preach with impunity. Some of the leading men of the Quraysh went in a deputation to Abu Talib. 'Your nephew,' they said, 'has declared our gods as false, he has accused us of error; either you must stop him or you must let us get at him, for you yourself are in the same position as we are in opposition to him and we will rid you of him.' He gave them a conciliatory answer and the crisis was averted. The Apostle's relations with the Quraysh continued to deteriorate till they went a second time to Abu Talib and said: 'You have a high and lofty position among us, and we have asked you to put a stop to your nephew's activities but you have not done so. By God, we cannot tolerate that our forefathers should be reviled, our customs mocked and our gods insulted. Until we are rid of him we will fight both of you till one side perishes.' Abu Talib was deeply distressed. He sent for his nephew and said: 'Spare me and yourself. Do not put on me a burden greater than I can bear.' The Apostle answered, 'By God, if they put the sun in my right hand and the moon in my left and ask me to abandon my mission, until God has made it victorious, or I perish therein, I would not abandon it.' The Apostle burst into tears, and got up. As he turned away, his uncle called him back and said, 'Go and say what you please, for by God I will never give you up on my account.'

The Quraysh perceived that Abu Talib would not give up his nephew. They adopted the only course left to them —inciting the people against the Apostle and his followers.

The whole of Arabia was now talking about Muhammad. A multitude of opinions were being expressed: He is a *Kahin* (a soothsayer). No, he is not, for he does not possess the gibberish and rhymed speech of the *Kahin*. He is possessed. No, he is not, for there is no choking, no spasmodic movements and no whisperings. He is a poet. No, he is not, because his utterances do not conform to the forms and metres of poetry. He is a sorcerer. No, he is not, for we have seen sorcerers and he does not spit or blow. He is a prophet, a messenger of God. No, he is not, for he is an illiterate man and an orphan at that. There were arguments in every fair. Much that Muhammad said was familiar and acceptable. His speech was sweet and reasonable and yet people were slow, very slow, to respond. On the contrary, his own people who were unanimous in acclaiming his unimpeachable honesty and integrity accused him of being a liar, a diviner, a poet, a man possessed. Persecution was let loose. Muhammad exercised the utmost restraint in the face of grave provocation.

With the conversion of Hamza[5] to Islam there was a change in tactics. 'Utba b. Rabi'a went to Muhammad with certain proposals for a *rapprochement*. 'Utba 'sat by the Prophet and said, "O my nephew, you are one of us as you know, of the nobles of the tribe. You have come to your people with an important matter, dividing their community thereby and ridiculing their customs, and you have insulted their gods and their religion, and declared that their forefathers were unbelievers, so listen to me and I will make some suggestions, and perhaps you will be able to accept one of them." The apostle agreed, and he went on, "If what you want is money, we will gather for you all our property so that you may be the richest of us; if you want honour, we will make you our chief so that no one can decide anything apart from you; if you want sovereignty, we will make you king, and if this ghost which comes to you, which you see, is such that you cannot get rid of him, we will find a physician for you, and exhaust our means in getting you cured. . . ." '[6] The Apostle listened patiently and then recited the Sura from the Qur'an: 'Our hearts are veiled from that to which you invite us.'[7] The Prophet continued to recite the Sura and ended at the words: 'Prostrate yourself to God'—and prostrated himself, and said, 'You have heard what you have heard, the rest remains with you.' When 'Utba returned to his companions, he told them that he had heard words such as he had never heard before, which were neither poetry, spells, nor sorcery. 'Take my advice and do as I do, leave this man entirely alone for, by God, the words which I have heard will be blazed abroad. If (other) Arabs kill him, others will have rid you of him; if he gets the better of the Arabs, his sovereignty will be your sovereignty, . . . and you will be prosperous through him.'[8]

The Quraysh, apprehensive of their own position, negotiated and argued with Muhammad. The arguments followed a familiar pattern. If it was money he wanted, they would make him the richest of all; if it was sovereignty, they would make him their chief. But the Prophet sought not money, nor honour, nor sovereignty. The debate continued. The Quraysh lost both their case and their temper. Every clan attacked its Muslims, imprisoned them, beat them, denied them food and drink, and exposed them to the gruelling heat of Mecca. And this treatment did not last a week, a month or a year; it continued for thirteen long years. The Prophet was by no means a young man with an extraordinary capacity for endurance; he was already fifty-three while he was still suffering in Mecca.

It was a painful plight that the Prophet faced in his home town. He prepared a plan to move out and try his luck in Ta'if—a town of proud chiefs who wielded great influence on Arab opinion. If only he could bring them around, he thought, he would have made a good beginning. But a bitter experience was in store for him. The people of the city turned out in their full strength to witness the spectacle of his humiliation. His rejection was both unceremonious and unqualified. Injury was added to insult. As Muhammad came out of his meeting with the chiefs who had turned down his invitation to Islam, he was faced on both sides of the road by a milling crowd which was not content with verbal abuse but which

followed it up with physical violence. The Prophet proceeded along the route at a pace which suggested that he
was not at all perturbed by the stones which were being
pelted at a distinguished visitor who at least deserved
the traditional hospitality so ungrudgingly accorded to
an ordinary Arab. Soon the path which the Prophet
treaded began to shed a trail of blood. The young ruffians
hit the Prophet, and hit him hard. Walking became difficult as his feet began to bleed from injuries inflicted by
his hosts who shouted with hilarity every time a stone hit
his feet. The rain of stones was accompanied by jeers
and abuse.

The reply to all the persecution was a prayer—a prayer
to God for guidance for those who knew not what they
did!

The tragedy of Ta'if was not the end of the struggle.
The Prophet was again on his feet. With faith in his
mission Muhammad persevered, even though alone. All
the odds were against him. There was a price on his head.
Thirteen years of persecution in Mecca failed to break
his spirit. His enemies became desperate at their own
failure to arrest the appeal of Islam. All the chiefs in
Mecca convened a conference to devise ways and means
to put an end to this menace. One of them suggested that
Muhammad should be chained and imprisoned in his
own house, another argued that exile would be the best
solution. Abu Jahl, however, suggested that a representative should be selected from each tribe and all of them
should then jointly put an end to the life of Muhammad,
the idea being that responsibility for his death should be
shared by all the tribes because the Hashimites alone
could not possibly face the consequences of the dastardly
crime. Abu Jahl's suggestion found favour with the
tribal chiefs. The Prophet's house was besieged by the

armed representatives of different tribes in Mecca before the sun had set on the town. According to Arab tradition it is unchivalrous to enter the women's apartments, and the tribal representatives stayed outside his house. At this time, when the Prophet's house was besieged, his first thought was not for his life but for the deposits left with him by the people of Mecca. He sent for 'Ali, his young cousin, and said to him, 'I have been commanded by God to leave for Medina and I shall leave tonight. You should sleep in my bed tonight and in the morning you should return all the deposits left with me by the people.' He then gave him the details of the articles left with him in addition to the names and addresses of the people who had deposited them with him.

The Prophet kept calm even while the sword was hanging over his head. The night came. The Quraysh stalwarts with swords who were patrolling outside his house, waiting for the Prophet to come out, had all fallen asleep when the Prophet came out. He cast a glance at Mecca and surveyed the place of his birth. 'Mecca!' he sighed, 'you are dearer to me than the whole world, but your sons will not permit me to live here!' He left his house and went to spend the rest of the night in the cave of Thaur with a devoted companion. He spent three nights in that cave. The whole of Mecca was indignant at his escape and every nook and corner was searched. A tracker led a party of the Quraysh to the very mouth of the cave. The Prophet and his companion could hear the voices outside as they sat in the dark cave waiting for an opportunity to pursue their journey in the heat of a hostile desert. These were moments of supreme anxiety. His companion expressed concern about the Prophet's safety. 'Be not afraid,' admonished the Prophet calmly, 'for verily God is with us.'[9]

THE FIRST TREATY OF ISLAM: COVENANT
WITH MEDINIANS AND THE JEWS

Muhammad migrated to Medina in the fifty-third year of his life. He had been driven out by his own people. Medina welcomed Muhammad with open arms. The Apostle was, however, perfectly clear in his mind that the basic structure of society was no different in Medina than it was in Mecca. The Arabs in both places suffered from a lack of leadership; this void was caused by their pride, conceit, ambition and endless rivalry for supremacy. The clan reigned supreme. Every clan vied with the others for securing the supremacy of the tribe. Few would suffer to remain under the domination of another man, no matter whether he was his own father, brother or a tribal chief; and they had many chiefs.[10]

The newcomer had, therefore, to reconcile a variety of conflicting interests if he was to avail himself of his new refuge as an effective centre from which he could direct his movement with comparative security. His first act, therefore, was to negotiate a treaty with the people of Medina and the Jews. This was the first treaty he ever signed. It is a document of great historical importance, not only because it is the first treaty in Islam but because it elaborates the revolutionary concept of a state the foundations of which are laid on faith but which bestows oneness of community on those who do not belong to the same faith but are loyal to it in the political sense. The Muslims are declared as one community (*ummah*) to the exclusion of all men. The bond which unites them is their common faith. The Muslims from Mecca became the brothers of Muslims from Medina, while they became enemies of their own real brothers who chose to stay behind in Mecca. Their friendship and their enmity is governed, therefore, not by considerations of common

ties of blood or economy, tribe or family, but by the
ideology which binds them together; it is their willingness to suffer and live together and pursue a common
way of life which lends them the consciousness of a community. And yet the Jews in Medina are accorded
equality—the word *equality* occurs time and again in the
treaty. They are not to be wronged nor are their enemies
to be aided. The Muslims have their faith, the Jews have
theirs. The freedom of religion is recognised and the
Jews of Banu 'Auf are declared as one community with
the believers. In addressing them after the signing of the
treaty the Prophet is reported to have said: 'Your flesh is
our flesh and your blood is our blood.' While they are
established in their religion and their property, the
reciprocal obligations are also stated. Besides, the document lays down general rules of conduct which appear
revolutionary even to this day to a student of diplomacy
unaccustomed to an ethical approach to national affairs.
The first treaty in Islam deserves to be carefully studied.
It runs as follows:

In the name of God, the Merciful, the Compassionate!
This is a writing of Muhammad the Prophet between
the believers and Muslims of (Meccan) Quraysh and
Yathrib and those who follow them and are attached to
them and who crusade (*jahadu*) along with them.
1. They are a single community (*ummah*) distinct
from (other) people.
2. The emigrants of Quraysh, according to their former
condition, pay jointly the blood-money between them, and
they (as a group) ransom their captive (s), (doing so)
with uprightness and justice between the believers.
3. Banu 'Auf, according to their former condition, pay
jointly the previous blood-wits, and each sub-clan (*ta'ifa*)
ransoms its captive (s), (doing so) with uprightness and
justice between the believers.

4. Banu Harith, according to their former condition, pay jointly . . .— (as 3).

    5. Banu Sa'idah . . .— (as 3).

    6. Banu Jusham . . .— (as 3).

    7. Banu al-Najjar . . .— (as 3).

    8. Banu 'Amr b. 'Auf . . .— (as 3).

    9. Banu al-Nabit . . .— (as 3).

  10. Banu al-Aus . . .— (as 3).

11. The believers do not forsake a debtor among them, but give him (help), according to what is fair, for ransom or blood-wit.

12. A believer does not take as confederate (halif) the client (maula) of a believer without his (the latter's) consent.

13. The God-fearing believers are against whoever of them acts wrongfully or seeks (plans) an act that is unjust or treacherous or hostile or corrupt among the believers; their hands are all against him, even if he is the son of one of them.

14. A believer does not kill a believer because of an unbeliever, and does not help an unbeliever against a believer.

15. The security (dhimmah) of God is one; the granting of 'neighbourly protection' (yujir) by the lowliest of them (the believers) is binding on them; the believers are protectors (or clients=mawali) of one another to the exclusion of (other) people.

16. Whoever of the Jews follows us has the (same) help and support (nasr, iswah) (as the believers) so long as they are not wronged (by him) and he does not help (others) against them.

17. The peace (silm) of the believers is one; no believer makes peace apart from another believer, where there is fighting in the way of God, except in so far as equality and justice between them (is maintained).

18. In every expedition made with us the parties take turns with one another.

19. The believers exact vengeance from one another where a man gives his blood in the way of God. The God-fearing believers are under the best and most correct guidance.

20. No idolater (*mushrik*) gives 'neighbourly protection' (*yujir*) for goods or person to Quraysh, nor intervenes in his (a Quraysh's) favour against a believer.

21. When anyone wrongly kills a believer, the evidence being clear, he is liable to be killed in retaliation for him, unless the heirs of the murdered man agree and are satisfied (with a payment). The believers are against him (the murderer) entirely; nothing is permissible to them except to oppose him.

22. It is not permissible for a believer who has agreed to what is in this document (*sahifa*) and believed in God and the last day to help a wrong-doer or give him shelter. If anyone helps him or gives him shelter, upon this man is the curse of God and His wrath on the day of Resurrection, and from him nothing will be accepted to make up for it or take its place.

23. Wherever there is anything about which you differ, it is to be referred to God and to Muhammad (peace be upon him).

24. The Jews share the expenses with the believers so long as they (Muslims) continue at war.

25. The Jews of Banu 'Auf are a separate community (*ummah*) as the believers. To the Jews their religion (*din*) and to the Muslims their faith. (This applies both to their clients and to themselves, with the exception of anyone who has done wrong or acted treacherously; he brings evil only on himself and on his household.)

26. For the Jews of Banu al-Najjar the like of what is for the Jews of Banu 'Auf.

27. For the Jews of Banu al-Harith the like. . . .

28. For the Jews of Banu Sa'idah the like. . . .

29. For the Jews of Banu Jusham the like. . . .

30. For the Jews of Banu al-Aus the like. . . .

31. For the Jews of Banu Tha'labah the like of what is for the Jews of Banu 'Auf, with the exception of anyone who has done wrong or acted treacherously; he brings evil only on himself and his household.

32. Jafnah, a sub-division (*batn*) of Tha'labah, are like them.

33. For Banu al-Shutaybah the like of what is for the Jews of Banu 'Auf; honourable dealing (comes) before treachery.

34. The clients (*mawali*) of Tha'labah are like them.

35. The *bitanah* of (particular) Jews are as themselves.

36. No one of the (? those belonging to the *ummah*) may go out (to war) without permission of Muhammad (peace be upon him), but he is not restrained from taking vengeance for wounds. Whoever acts rashly (*fataka*), it (involves) only himself and his household, except where a man has been wronged. God is the truest (fulfiller) of this (document).

37. It is for the Jews to bear their expenses and for the Muslims to bear their expenses. Between them (that is, to one another) there is help (*nasr*) against whoever wars against the people of this document. Between them is sincere friendship (*nas'h wa nasihah*), and honourable dealing, not treachery. A man is not guilty of treachery through (the act of) his confederate. There is help for (or, help is to be given to) the person wronged.

38. The Jews bear expenses along with the believers so long as they continue at war.

39. The valley of Yathrib is sacred for the people of this document.

40. The 'protected neighbour' (*jar*) is as the man himself so long as he does not harm and does not act treacherously.

41. No woman is given 'neighbourly protection' (*najr*) without the consent of her people.

42. Whenever among the people of this document there occurs any incident (disturbance) or quarrel from which

disaster for it (the people) is to be feared, it is to be referred to God and to Muhammad, the Messenger of God (God bless and preserve him). God is the most scrupulous and truest (fulfiller) of what is in this document.

43. No 'neighbourly protection' is given (la tujar) to the Quraysh and those who help them.

44. Between them (? the people of this document) is help against whoever suddenly attacks Yathrib.

45. Whenever they are summoned to conclude and accept a treaty, they conclude and accept it; when they in turn summon to the like of that, it is for them upon the believers, except whoever war about religion; for (?= incumbent on) each man is his share from their side which is towards them.

46. The Jews of al-Aus, both their clients and themselves, are in the same position as belongs to the people of this document while they are thoroughly honourable in their dealings with the people of this document. Honourable dealing (comes) before treachery.

47. A person acquiring (? guilt) acquires it only against himself. God is the most upright and truest fulfiller of what is in this document. This writing does not intervene to protect a wrong-doer or traitor. He who goes out is safe, and he who sits still is safe in Medina, except whoever does wrong and acts treacherously. God is 'protecting neighbour' (jar) of him who acts honourably and fears God, and Muhammad is the Messenger of God (God bless and preserve him).

This treaty is so important that it is usually referred to as the 'Constitution of Medina.' It sets out clearly the ideas underlying the Islamic State in its early formative years. It explicitly states that disputes are to be referred to Muhammad. Montgomery Watt rightly points out[11] that the provision that disputes were to be referred to the Prophet would not itself increase his power, unless he had sufficient tact and diplomacy to find a settlement that would command general agreement. It is on record that far from being an autocratic ruler of Medina, Muhammad initiated a system of consultations and decided almost all major issues after taking the leading companions into his confidence. The treaty places an overwhelming emphasis on the unity of the *ummah* in war and peace. The revolutionary nature of this concept is best understood by reference to the narrow tribal outlook of the Arabs before Islam.

To an Arab his own tribe represented all that was most worthwhile in life. All members of a tribe acted as one man and were united in the defence of a fellowtribesman, regardless of the nature of his crime; for when an individual committed a crime, the whole tribe not only endorsed his action but also shared responsibility with him. 'Our tribesmen, wrong or right,' seemed to be the motto. 'We do not ask our brothers,' says a poet, 'for reasons and explanations (for a crime) when he appeals for help.' On the contrary, it was an accepted principle of morality that the actions of a fellow-tribesman directed against another must be endorsed by the whole tribe, which should bear complete responsibility for the consequences. In cases, however, where a man failed to get this protection, he left the tribe and joined another which undertook to offer him asylum. The Bedouin patriotism was, therefore, neither national nor territorial; it was strictly tribal. It was loyalty to the tribe alone which mattered; and no tribe which failed to protect a member could command this loyalty. 'Be loyal to the tribe,' sang a bard; 'its claim upon its members is strong enough to make a husband give up his wife.'

The tribal morality was a constant source of friction. Attack, counterattack, loot and plunder, revenge and vendetta were the evils inherent in the very system of Bedouin life. Blood called for blood, and a blood-feud could last for forty years. When there were no storms to brave, the Bedouin found the period of calm repugnant to his mercurial nature. The calm was never for him a temptation for quietly settling down; it always provided him with an opportunity for brewing a new storm! And when he could find no enemy to deal with, he found an outlet for his irresistible urge for fighting in attacking his own people, for attack he must, even if the victim be a brother! Al-Qutami, the Arab poet of the early Umayyad period, has beautifully summed up this guiding principle of a Bedouin's life: 'Our business is to make raids on the enemy, on our neighbour and our own brother, in case we find none to raid but a brother.'

Romantic indeed was the moral code of the Bedouin, and its essence can perhaps be expressed in the word *chivalry,* or *Muru'ah* as the Arab calls it. The virtues and vices of the Bedouin, his devotion to his clan, his sense of honour together with his recklessness, thirst for revenge and his disregard for human life have been portrayed forcefully and faithfully by eminent writers like Burton and Lane-Poole. Most unscrupulous in raids on the enemy, the Bedouin set himself exacting standards of courage and hospitality. Courage was determined by the number of men he killed or engaged in a raid or by the valour he displayed in defending his own tribe against an enemy. A good 'knight' was expected to be first on the battlefield and last in claiming his booty. Hospitality was judged by the number of camels he slaughtered for a guest, or by the generosity he showed towards the poor and the needy. Arab hospitality often led to excesses in eating and drinking. It was considered with some a point of honour to remain in a tavern until the wine merchant was compelled to take down his sign, the wine being spent!

The Arab was incapable even of comprehending the

concept of a world beyond the frontiers of his clan. The Jazirat al-Arab—the island of Arabia—was indeed an island in the true sense of the word. With the rise of Islam the isolated Arab was brought face to face for the first time with the realities of the world outside his own narrow domain of the clan, and he soon found himself on the way to conquering a large part of the known world. The conception of the dominance of the sovereign and independent political entity, called the tribe, had been based essentially on kinship. The concept of the *ummah* was, however, based on religion. The Prophet is the head and director of the *ummah*. In later treaties, as in the Constitution of Medina, it is always the security of God and Muhammad that is invoked. The enemies of the *ummah* are essentially the unbelievers and the idolaters. It is not on the basis of kinship but on the basis of a common faith that the *ummah* thrives and the prohibition of intermarriage with pagans is a significant factor. All members of the *ummah* are equally protected, all are equally capable of giving protection which the whole *ummah* is obliged to accept as a collective responsibility. They all stand to one another in the relation of protector and protected, while none is to be protected, except temporarily, by anyone outside the community.

The treaty abolished the local, territorial and tribal alliances so conspicuous in the history of Arabia. The principle that 'there is no confederacy (*hilf*) in Islam' was accepted. No two groups within the community were to establish a specially close relationship, for this would amount to a denial of Islam and would imply that the protection given by Muhammad or his successors was incomplete. The subdivisions into which tribal Arabia was divided became redundant in theory. The movement of unification started by this treaty was amply justified by later events which showed that Islam was capable not only of doing away with divisions and subdivisions but of expanding itself into an efficient and effective commonwealth and a living force.

THE BATTLE OF BADR

The Treaty of Medina was by no means to mark the end of Muhammad's troubles. It only marked the end of a phase and the beginning of another. His compatriots of Mecca who persecuted him in his home town did not permit him to live in peace even in exile, which in fact provoked them to pursue their plans with added vigour. Muhammad in Medina was threatened both from within and without. The Jews who were very powerful in Medina constituted an internal danger while the Quraysh rallied their forces to assault him from without. The Prophet was caught in a web of intrigue and violence. He proceeded to enter into treaties and alliances with the Jews and several other tribes in the vicinity of Medina, but before he had time to secure many allies, the Quraysh were knocking at the gates of Medina. The Prophet's position can be judged by the fact that the forces of Islam could not muster more than 313 men to face the formidable foe in the battle of Badr.[12] Their plight was indeed pitiable. While they faced the forces of the Quraysh in the front, they feared the stab of the Jews in the back. The odds were heavily against them. It was during this crisis that two Muslims managed to reach the Apostle's camp after a successful escape from pagan Mecca. They were intercepted on the way by the Quraysh who released them after obtaining a pledge that the two Muslims would not take up arms against the Quraysh in the battle of Badr. But on reaching Medina they saw for themselves that the battle, which was being

fought with a handful of men, was a veritable struggle for
life and death. The addition of every single person
mattered. The Prophet himself had taken up arms in
order to add to the lean ranks of Islam. Having seen this
desperate situation, the two Muslim fugitives volunteered
their services to the Prophet. He firmly declined the offer
and advised them to return, for he could not possibly
suffer his followers to dishonour their undertaking under
any circumstances. The result was as spectacular as it
was unexpected. The Muslims secured a signal victory
over the Quraysh. But having won the victory over their
oppressors, the Muslims rose once again to greater heights
of honour and magnanimity in dealing with them. All
temptation of revenge was eschewed, and all considerations of personal injury were scrupulously subordinated
to the demands of peace and justice.

THE BATTLE OF UHUD

But the Quraysh, instead of appreciating this treatment,
were up again in a year's time to avenge their defeat in
the battle of Badr. Their numbers had swollen. The fight
in the battle of Uhud[13] was fierce. The scales seemed to
weigh evenly and at one time they seemed to turn clearly
in favour of the foes of Islam. This was a moment of
great trial. There was treachery on the part of 300 'hypocrites' led by 'Abdullah b. Ubayy,[14] who deserted. This
was a serious blow in the midst of battle, but the last straw
came when the Muslim archers in their impatience hur-
ried down the hill in pursuit of booty. They had imag-
ined that the victory was decisive. In violation of their
instructions they left their post of duty and reached for
a share of the booty in the plain below. The retreating
Quraysh could not have hoped for a better opportunity.

They returned and launched a relentless attack on the scattered Muslim forces which were taken by surprise. There was serious hand-to-hand fighting in which numbers told heavily in favour of the enemy. Many Muslims were killed[15] but there was no rout. The Prophet was wounded in the head and face and one of his front teeth was knocked out. He was now the main target of attack— a commander paying for the impatience of his men. With bleeding wounds he persevered in the fight. In spite of his wounds, he returned to the field next day to pursue the enemy. Many of the wounded Muslims, inspired by his example, followed suit. In the face of this determination on the part of the Muslims, the Meccan army thought it prudent to withdraw.

The same spirit of perseverance prevailed when the Prophet was called once again to defend Medina against the threat of a united confederacy of Arab tribes. The siege lasted about a month and men in the town were groaning with hunger. With a brace of stones tied over his stomach, the Prophet stood up against both the onslaughts of hunger and the hordes of the confederates. Patience could not have been taxed more, but Muhammad's store was inexhaustible. He scored once again over thousands. He did not lose patience even with those who had attempted to exterminate him. He continued to extend his hand of friendship to them in the hope that tolerance and kindness would win where force and intimidation were sure to fail.

THE TREATY OF HUDAYBIYA

There is a wealth of material on Muhammad's dealings with the Quraysh, but it is by no means our intention to deal exhaustively with it. Our object is merely to touch on representative incidents. By far the greatest achievement of the Apostle, in his dealings with the Quraysh, was the part played by him in negotiating the Treaty of Hudaybiya six years after his migration from Mecca.

The scene is Hudaybiya—a small village to the north of Mecca, from which it is easily reached in a short day's march. The time is February 628. Some fourteen hundred men have encamped in the plain under the leadership of Muhammad, the Prophet of Islam, who was driven out of Mecca six years earlier by the Quraysh. There is a time-honoured custom to visit unarmed the Sacred Enclosure of the Ka'ba, where fighting of any kind is prohibited during the Sacred Months which include the month of Dhi-Qa'da. It was in this month that the Prophet led a caravan of fourteen hundred of his followers from Medina to perform the 'Umra or the little pilgrimage. To all intents and purposes no violation of the law was involved and the Arabs from Medina were perfectly entitled to avail themselves of a right which was freely enjoyed by all the Arabs. But the Arab tribes of Mecca, contrary to all traditions and expectations, decided suddenly to deny the right of entry to the Arabs from Medina. This was an unwarranted departure from the established convention which had prevailed since the days of Abraham. But, then, Muhammad and his followers had to suffer this discrimination because they had departed from the religion of their ancestors. The Arabs of Mecca had decided to throw down the gauntlet. Khalid b. Walid, who was later to become one of the most distinguished generals of Islam, was one of the ringleaders of this movement which rallied all the tribes in Mecca to give battle to the intended pilgrims from Medina. The Prophet came to know of these hostile preparations through Badil, a leader of the Khuza'ah tribe in Mecca, who, although not yet a Muslim, was sympathetically inclined towards Muslims. Through him the Prophet sent word to the Quraysh, the guardians of the Ka'ba, assuring them that he had come on a pilgrimage and that he had no designs of war. During the six years of the Prophet's stay in Medina, the Quraysh had been seriously depleted in numbers. Muhammad took this opportunity to propose a treaty of peace for a fixed period; and what if the offer was refused? 'By God, Who holds my life in His hand,' he said, 'I shall fight so long as there is a head on my shoulders.' This, then, was a message which offered peace with honour. But the Arabs of Mecca had taken a unilateral decision which they considered irrevocable. They declined to listen to the Prophet's message and would not be persuaded to do so till 'Urwa, a very old and revered Quraysh leader, intervened in the name of old age. 'Am I not your father and are you not my children,' he asked the angry Arabs of Mecca, 'and am I not firm in my integrity and loyalty to you?' He succeeded in pacifying the Arabs who gave him 'full powers' to negotiate with the Prophet, whose message, he believed, contained an offer of fair peace. 'Urwa came to negotiate with Muhammad. He sat before the Apostle and said: 'Muhammad, have you collected a mixed people together and then brought them to your own people to destroy them? The Quraysh have come out with their milch-camels, clad in leopard skins, swearing that you shall never enter Mecca by force. By God, I think I see you deserted by these people here tomorrow.' Abu Bakr was sitting behind the Apostle. He did not like 'Urwa's estimate of the loyalty of Muhammad's camp and used strong language in reiterating confidence in the Apostle's leadership. 'Urwa asked who had spoken and when he learned it was Abu Bakr, he said, 'By Allah, did I not owe you a favour I would pay you back for that, but now we are quits.' Then he began to take hold of his hand as he talked and advanced menacingly towards the Prophet's beard. Al-Mughira b. Shu'ba was standing by the Apostle, his head clad in mail; he began to hit 'Urwa's hand as he held the Apostle's beard saying, 'Take your hand away from the Apostle's face before you lose it.' 'Urwa said, 'Confound you, how rough and rude you are!' The Apostle smiled and told 'Urwa what he had told the other envoys of the Quraysh, namely, that he had not come out for war. 'Urwa got up from the Apostle's presence having seen how his companions treated him. Whenever he performed his ablutions they ran to get the water he had used; if a hair of his head fell they ran to pick it up. So he returned to the Quraysh and said, 'I have been to Chosro in his kingdom, and Caesar in his kingdom and the Negus in his kingdom, but never have I seen a king among a people like Muhammad among his companions. I have seen a people who will never abandon him for any reason, so form your own opinion.'

The discussions, which had remained inconclusive, had to be resumed. But 'Urwa, who had gone to Mecca for consultations, did not return. The Prophet sent an emissary to the Quraysh, who killed the camel on which he rode to them. The camel belonged to the Prophet himself who had placed it at the disposal of the envoy. But for the intervention of the more sober elements among the Quraysh, the envoy might have met the same fate as his camel. The insult was followed by injury when the Quraysh set out a force to attack the Muslims. Their soldiers, however, were captured by the Muslims and a battle was averted. Instead of thinking in terms of retaliation for the treatment meted out by his foes, the Prophet persisted in his plans of peace as if nothing had happened at all on the other side.

The Arabs of Mecca were clearly guilty of a breach of faith. Not only that: by committing an act of aggression against the Muslims while negotiations were still in progress between the two parties, they had unmistakably rejected the offer of peace. But the Prophet preserved his calm in the face of provocation, and instead of seeking the traditional Arab revenge he freed all the prisoners captured by his men and decided to proceed with his project of peace. It is to this decision that the Qur'an refers in these words:

> And He it is Who hath withheld men's hands from you, and hath withheld your hands from them, in the valley of Mecca, after He had made you victors over them. Allah is Seer of what ye do.[16]

Notwithstanding the treatment meted out earlier to his envoy, the Prophet sent 'Uthman b. 'Affan,[17] one of his closest associates, to resume the negotiations in Mecca. The Quraysh detained the envoy. This was, however, not known in the Muslim camp, and a rumour spread after some days of waiting that 'Uthman had been killed. This was the limit. Any further concession was bound to be considered a sign of weakness. The Prophet decided to avenge the blood of his envoy. Sitting under a tree in the plain of Hudaybiya, he demanded a covenant of fealty from all his followers. The response was spontaneous. Men and women who had followed their leader to perform a pilgrimage to Mecca now came forward to declare their determination to lay down their lives for the cause. The unique enthusiasm shown by that multitude united in devotion to their leader was evidence of the power he commanded. But the Quraysh had learned by six years' bitter experience that their power was crumbling on all sides and that Islam was growing with a moral and spiritual force which was clearly reflected in its capacity for organisation and resistance. No sooner had the Muslims announced their resolve to accept the challenge than they received the envoy of the Quraysh who came to resume negotiations for peace. The discussion stage being over, terms of settlement were reduced to writing. The draft treaty offered a number of obstacles, and the Prophet, who had already exhibited exemplary patience throughout the crisis, now rose to incredible heights of diplomacy in handling an extremely dangerous and delicate situation.

The opening sentence of the draft treaty was strongly objected to by Suhayl, the envoy of the Quraysh. This sentence did not contain the substance of the agreement; it only marked the usual beginning of any piece of writing by a Muslim. The draft began 'In the name of God, Most Gracious, Most Merciful,'[18] a beginning unacceptable to the Quraysh, whose envoy insisted that the sentence be replaced by the traditional formula of the Quraysh, who always prefaced all writings with the words 'In your name, O God.'[19] Both sentences conveyed the same meaning, but one had associations with the age-old tradition of the Quraysh and the other with the rising tradition of Islam. Suhayl insisted on his own form and the Prophet accepted it.

The nature and weight of the compromise agreed to by the Prophet in this case can be understood only if we make a brief reference to the gravity of the issues involved in substituting the word *Allah* for the word *Rahman* in the opening formula in the treaty of Hudaybiya. The word *Allah* was familiar to the Quraysh, though their concept of God was fundamentally different from the Prophet's concept of the One and Only God, for Allah was the name of the highest God acknowledged by the Quraysh; and when the message of Islam was preached in His name by the Prophet, it did not come to them as a complete surprise. Every time, however, the word *Rahman* was uttered in the same breath as Allah, the Quraysh reacted strongly against it, for they thought that Muhammad was trying to invent a new God called *Rahman* instead of Allah, whom they had known so well. The antipathy of the Quraysh to the use of the word *Rahman* is proved conclusively from the traditions, and we know it from Ibn Hisham's treatment of the battle of Badr, where Umayya b. Khalaf was fighting with 'Abd al-Rahman ibn 'Auf, who was one of the first six converts to Islam. Since the Quraysh refused fanatically to acknowledge Rahman, Umayya ibn Khalaf, though he was in danger of losing his life at Badr, refused to call 'Abd al-Rahman by his new name, as it implied recognition of Rahman, the name of God! He therefore shouted for him by his pagan name 'Abd 'Amr and not 'Abd al-Rahman! This prejudice has been referred to at various places in the Holy Qur'an.[20] Time and again the Qur'an makes references to the Quraysh's objection to the recognition of God by the name of Rahman. What is Rahman?[21] they ask. The Prophet answers them by saying: Call Him Allah or Rahman; by whatever name He (God) is called, to Him belong all the beautiful names. The Quraysh should therefore not object to the use of the word *Rahman,* for it gives expression to the concept of Allah, a word with which they are more familiar.

'Call upon Allah or call upon Rahman; whichever you call upon, He has the best names.'[22] No reason, however, was good enough to convince them, and they adhered to their own formula and would not agree to sign the Treaty of Hudaybiya because it began with the Muslim formula in which they seriously objected to the use of the word *Rahman.* The representative of the Quraysh—Suhayl—

insisted on his own form. The Prophet gave in, although for years conflict had been going on in which it was the endeavour of the Prophet to explain to the Quraysh the significance of the word *Rahman*.

This, then, was a compromise offered by the Prophet in the cause of peace. In offering the compromise, however, the Prophet did not depart from any basic principle vital to the integrity of Islam.

But there was another hurdle, far more formidable and fundamental in nature. The treaty was stated as having been agreed to by 'Muhammad, the Apostle of God.' The envoy of the Quraysh raised an objection to this expression, for if the Quraysh were to accept Muhammad as an apostle, there would be no quarrel between the two. They could not therefore accept that status being legalised in the form of a treaty and insisted on the deletion of the expression 'Apostle of God.' This was indeed a delicate matter and created a stir among the followers of the Prophet, who had suffered untold miseries, privations and persecutions only because they bore witness to the fact that there was no god but God and that Muhammad was His Apostle. This was no mere formula nor empty words; this was a declaration of faith which distinguished a Muslim from the unbeliever; and this was a point to defend which no Muslim would hesitate to sacrifice his life. Were they now to witness, without any emotion, the repudiation of the *raison d'etre* of their life? The fate of the tortuous negotiations now seemed to hang by a thread. Here was a predicament and a problem which required the highest qualities of confidence, clarity, tact and judgment. Here was a development which demanded a correct assessment of the situation on both sides—a clear decision capable of securing peace without sacrificing the interests of Islam. The Prophet rose equal to the situation and ordered the expression in question to be expunged. 'By God,' he declared, 'I am the Apostle of God, even though you believe not my claim.' And having clearly established that he had by no means renounced his claim to prophethood, he proceeded to order 'Ali, the scribe of the treaty, to put down his name as Muhammad, son of 'Abdullah. This was a difficult order, even for the most devoted follower, and for a while 'Ali hesitated to comply with it. The Prophet asked him to point out the place in the draft where the expression 'Apostle of God' occurred. 'Ali placed his finger on the spot and the Prophet himself erased the expression. Thus came to be finalised the Treaty of Hudaybiya, which offers a most rewarding study of the Prophet as a diplomat not only in the circumstances leading to its conclusion but also in the substance of the treaty, which was responsible for the final victory of Islam over the pagan Quraysh.

The Treaty of Hudaybiya stipulated that the Muslims should return to Medina without performing the pilgrimage; they could come the next year for this purpose but should return after three days' stay in Mecca; they should come unarmed for the pilgrimage though Muslim pilgrims were permitted to carry one sheathed sword each; if from Mecca a male Quraysh, under guardianship, should submit to the Prophet without the guardian's permission, he should be sent back to the guardian, but on the contrary a Muslim was not to be sent back to Medina; there was to be a truce between the parties for ten years; and any tribe or person was free to join either party or make an alliance with it.

This is how the document reads:

With Thy name, O God! This is what was agreed upon between Muhammad, son of 'Abdullah, and Suhayl, son of 'Amr.

They both agreed to put down fighting on the part of people for ten years, during which period the people were to enjoy peace and refrain from fighting with each other.

And whereas whoever of the companions of Muhammad comes to Mecca in Hajj or 'Umra pilgrimage, or in quest of the bounty of God (i.e. commerce, cf. Qur'an, lxii. 10), enroute to Yemen or Ta'if, such shall be in security regarding his person or property. And whoever comes to Medina, from among the Quraysh, enroute to Syria or Iraq (variat: Egypt) seeking the bounty of God, such shall be in security regarding his person and property.

And whereas whoever comes to Muhammad from among the Qurayshites without the permission of his guardian (*maula*), he (i.e. the Prophet) will hand him over to them; and whoever comes to the Quraysh from among those who are with Muhammad, they will not hand him over to him.

And that between us is a tied-up breast (i.e. bound to fulfil the terms), and that there shall be no secret help violating neutrality, and no acting unfaithfully.

And that whosoever likes to enter the league of Muhammad and his alliance may enter into it; and whosoever likes to enter the league of the Quraysh and their alliance may enter it.

And that thou (Muhammad) shalt return from us (Quraysh) in this year and enter not in our midst; and that when it is the coming year, we shall go out from thee and thou shalt enter with thy companions and stay there three nights, with thee being the weapon of the rider: having swords at the side; thou shalt not enter with what is other than them (swords).

And that the animals of sacrifice (brought by thee) will be slaughtered where we found them (i.e. in Hudaybiya), and thou shalt not conduct them to us (in Mecca).

[Probably Seal of Muhammad and Seal of Suhayl]
WITNESSES:
Muslims: Abu Bakr, 'Umar, 'Abd al-Rahman ibn 'Auf,

'Abdullah ibn Suhayl ibn 'Amr, Sa'd ibn Abi
Waqqas, Muhammad ibn Maslamah, etc.
Meccans: Mikrad ibn Hafs, etc.
SCRIBE AND WITNESS: 'Ali ibn Abi Talib.

Two copies of the treaty were prepared. One was
kept by the Prophet, and the other was handed over to
Suhayl, the plenipotentiary of the Quraysh.[23]
The whole treaty reads like a story of concessions. It
gives an impression more of surrender than of peace
with honour. The clause which laid down that any male
from Mecca who sought refuge with the Prophet was to
be extradited while no reciprocal measures were to be
taken by the Meccan Quraysh roused deep indignation
among the Muslims. On the face of it, the whole document reads like a treaty imposed on the vanquished by
a conqueror who has won a clear victory in the battlefield. This, at least, was the feeling in the Muslim camp,
which was visibly dejected and disappointed. When the
treaty was being signed in Hudaybiya, there was nothing
but deep disappointment in the Muslim camp, which,
but for its unflinching loyalty to the Apostle, would have
risen in protest against what was apparently a most
humiliating arrangement. The Muslims had bound themselves to return Arabs from Mecca to the Quraysh—how
this clause was to operate to the detriment of Muslims
became obvious while Suhayl, the envoy of the Quraysh,
was still in Hudaybiya. His own son, Abu Jandal, who
had embraced Islam and was being subjected to tortures
in imprisonment in Mecca on that account, managed
somehow to escape from the Quraysh and reached the
Muslim camp still in chains. Here, then, are present all
the ingredients of a spectacular drama. Abu Jandal is a
Muslim. He has suffered untold miseries on that account.

He falls at the feet of the Prophet and begs for protection and asylum. He shows his body, blue with injuries inflicted on him by the enemies of Islam, and entreats the Muslims not to hurl him back into the jaws of death. The whole Muslim camp, already downcast with a sense of frustration, is shocked to the core, and their sympathy for Abu Jandal, their brother-in-faith, is roused to a high pitch. Here was a test case which demanded the highest measure of integrity; the slightest wavering of one's mind could have set at naught all that was achieved through a process of slow and painful negotiations under trying circumstances. While Abu Jandal pleaded for protection, his father, who was none else than the envoy of the Quraysh, sternly demanded his immediate surrender under the terms of the treaty. No less a person than 'Umar entreated the Prophet, on behalf of the Muslims, to offer protection to Abu Jandal, but Muhammad decided to stand by his word. In a voice charged with emotion he counselled patience to Abu Jandal and ordered him to return with his captor—his own father. Abu Jandal[24] shrieked at the top of his voice, 'Am I to be returned to the polytheists that they may entice me from my religion?' The Apostle said, 'O Abu Jandal, be patient and control yourself, for God will provide relief and a means of escape for you and those of you who are helpless. We have made peace with them, we and they have invoked God in our agreement, and we cannot deal falsely with them.' Umar jumped up and walked alongside Abu Jandal, saying, 'Be patient, for they are only polytheists; the blood of one of them is but the blood of a dog,' and brought the hilt of his sword close up to him. 'Umar used to say that he had hoped that Abu Jandal would take the sword and kill his father with it, but the man spared his father and carried out the command of the Apostle.

The decision to return a Muslim to the Quraysh cast a cloud of gloom over the entire Muslim camp. With heavy hearts and hanging heads, Muslims, conscious of their helplessness, saw their brother being handed back to their enemies—the first instance of this nature in the history of Islam. But they bore it with a fortitude characteristic of the followers of the Prophet. Their cup was full to the brim and was indeed overflowing. The last straw came when the Prophet ordered the slaughter of the animals which the Muslims had brought with them for purposes of ritual sacrifice connected with the pilgrimage. It appeared too much of a joke to offer the sacrifice without being able to perform the pilgrimage from which they had been prevented by the Quraysh. It was a sad and sorry reminder of their defeat. So deep was the sense of frustration that the Prophet thrice repeated his directions, but none of his followers could muster the necessary spirit of good cheer so essential for offering a sacrifice. It was only after the Prophet took the lead that the rest followed. The whole camp returned from Hudaybiya three days after the signing of the treaty, and while they were marching back to Medina, a multitude of men whose morale was at the lowest possible ebb, their heads hanging in gloom and their hearts cast in grief, they were told in the words of the Qur'an: 'Lo! We have given thee (O Muhammad) a signal victory.'[25] A signal victory? What, then, is defeat if this be called a victory?—asked the sceptics. And yet this treaty which seemed so completely to disappoint the followers of the Prophet was to prove the very foundation on which the edifice of Islam was to be raised in the years to come. But while the leader had vision and had clearly anticipated the course of coming events, even the best of his followers were so much lost in the mood of the moment that they failed to grasp its effect on the future of Islam.

'Umar, who was one of the bitter critics of the Treaty of Hudaybiya, was later to repent for his views.

It is easy to be wise after the event, but at the time of signing the treaty the best among Muslim leaders failed to perceive the effect of the agreement. Before the treaty, Muslims had no means of contact with Mecca. With the conclusion of a treaty of peace they secured free access to it. This made all the difference to the cause of Islam. The period intervening between the Treaty of Hudaybiya in A.H. 6 and the conquest of Mecca in A.H. 8 is the most fruitful period of Islam, for it brought to its fold the largest number of Muslims in Mecca before its final surrender. The commanders who were later to conquer Syria and Egypt for Islam—Khalid b. al-Walid and 'Amr b. al-'As—were the fruit of this period of contact between Medina and Mecca. The clause which created the greatest measure of dismay in the Muslim camp was the provision without which this result could not have been possible. Muslims sent back to Mecca were not likely to renounce Islam; on the other hand, they would act by their example as influential centres of Islam. Few could see at that time that it was more important to ensure that Muslims should be allowed to remain in Mecca than that they should be sent back to Medina. The Quraysh were obviously unaware of these implications; and when the clause started operating to their own detriment in winning over converts to Islam, they took the initiative in modifying it and agreed that it should cease to operate. This opened the way for Muslims held as prisoners in Mecca to proceed to Medina. Abu Jandal, whose plight had nearly wrecked the Treaty of Hudaybiya, was one of the beneficiaries of this amendment. Hudaybiya, then, was a great victory, moral and social as well as political, and its lessons are expounded in the Qur'an in a Sura which is significantly called 'Victory.'

In Hudaybiya we see the Prophet as a diplomat: a negotiator with a clear vision and firm grasp on the essentials of his objective; a man who can hold his own under the most trying circumstances; a man who can preserve his calm and maintain his balance in the face of disturbing provocations; an ambassador completely devoted to ideals of peace and dedicated to winning it without sacrificing the dignity of man; a diplomat who knows when to be firm, when to give way, when to temporise and when to build bridges for a retreat. Here we see the unique combination of visionary and practical man. Surrounded by a surging sea of emotionalism, he rises to rare heights of objectivity and uses language which in contrast to his surroundings appears amazingly staid and devoid of all sensationalism and overstatement. With an unerring instinct he analyses in a flash the strengths and failings of his own people and proceeds in a quick, unostentatious manner to negotiate and obtain the best possible treaty which is a model of foresight, tact, patience, faith and judgment. Despite the dissatisfaction of some of his companions and followers who did not then realise the advantages gained, he agreed not to add his title of 'Apostle of God' to his name in the document when it stood in the way of its ratification by the Meccans. But, on the other hand, he knew how to wrest from the opponents what he had set his heart upon, and thus he dealt with Mecca on equal terms and in the capacity of head of state.

MUHAMMAD'S CONDUCT AS THE CONQUEROR OF MECCA

The Treaty of Hudaybiya paved the way for the greatest single event in the history of early Islam. It is the 20th

of Ramadan, the month in which Muhammad received
his first revelation in the cave of Hira in the same town.
The man who was driven out of Mecca returns home at
the head of a victorious army. The haughty Quraysh are
outwitted and outnumbered. Mecca has been taken by
surprise. There is panic among the people of Mecca. The
Muslim soldiers are passing through the streets in small
batches with their standards. Finally comes the Apostle
with his greenish-black squadron in which are included
Muhajirs and Ansar whose eyes alone are visible because
of their armour. Sa'd, one of the commanders, is reported
to have said:

> Today is the day of war,
> Sanctuary is no more!

There is fear and trepidation. The people of Mecca
are certain that the hour of revenge has come. They are
well aware of the treatment they had meted out over a
period of thirteen years to the Prophet and his followers.
They are mentally preparing themselves for the retribu-
tion which they are sure will come. The whole population
of Mecca, deeply conscious of its guilt, is trembling in its
shoes. In this population are some of the inveterate foes
of Muhammad and Islam. Here lives that ferocious
woman Hind who tore the liver from the corpse of the
Prophet's own uncle, and here live the people who inflicted tortures on the Prophet and his followers. Now
that they lie vanquished at his feet, how is Muhammad
going to settle his scores with them?

At the supreme moment of victory, Muhammad,
turbaned with a piece of red Yamani cloth, halted on his
horse and lowered his head in submission to God, his
beard almost touching the middle of the saddle. When
he entered the town he was preceded by a herald who

cried at the top of his voice: 'O Quraysh, this is Muhammad, who has come to you with a force you cannot resist. He who enters Abu Sufyan's house is safe and he who locks himself up is safe and he who enters the Mosque is safe.' Who is this Abu Sufyan? A prominent enemy of Islam who approached the Muslim camp on the eve of the conquest of Mecca and was escorted to the Prophet's presence. 'Umar demanded the penalty of death for his past record, but the Prophet not only granted him amnesty but also granted amnesty to those who chose to enter his house.

In an address to the citizens of Mecca, Muhammad reminded them of what they had done to him and his followers. What, then, he said, did the people of Mecca expect of him now that he had entered Mecca as a conqueror? There was a brief pause—a moment of suspense which held the lives of thousands in precarious balance. One of the Quraysh chiefs said: 'We know you are generous, and we expect you to treat us as a generous brother would.' The Apostle 'stood at the door of the Ka'ba and said: "There is no God but Allah alone; He has no associate. He has made good His promise and helped His servant. He has put to flight the confederates alone. Every claim of privilege or blood or property are [sic] abolished by me except the custody of the temple and the watering of the pilgrims. . . . O Quraysh, God has taken from you the haughtiness of paganism and its veneration of ancestors. Man springs from Adam and Adam sprang from dust." Then he read to them this verse: "O men, We created you from male and female and made you into peoples and tribes that you may know one another: of a truth the most noble of you in God's sight is the most pious." Then he added: ". . . What do you think that I am about to do with you?" They replied, "Good. You are a noble brother, son of a noble

brother." [26] The Prophet declared: 'Go! You are re-
lieved; no more responsibility burdens you to-day; you
are the freed ones.'

Thus he let them go, though they had done him
grievous wrong and he now had power over their lives.
Then the people gathered to do him homage. Muhammad sat on al-Safa while 'Umar remained below him im-
posing conditions on the people who paid homage to the
Apostle promising to hear and obey God and His Apostle
to the best of their ability. This applied to the men; when
they had finished he dealt with the women. Among the
Quraysh women who came was Hind b. 'Utba who came
veiled and disguised, for she was afraid that the Apostle
would punish her for her savage and ferocious treatment
of Hamza,[27] the Prophet's uncle. The treatment by
Muhammad, the conqueror of Mecca, of Hind b. 'Utba,
one of the thousands of humble vanquished women, is
symbolic of the attitude of clemency shown by the Apostle
at the hour of his triumphant entry into his native town.
Hind and her husband were the leading figures among
his persecutors; the husband Abu Sufyan had accepted
Islam a short while before the fall of Mecca but to Hind
the Apostle owed no protection; he had, on the contrary,
a number of scores to settle with her, the worst being her
treatment of Hamza. The Prophet recognised her voice
and having done so did not utter a word about the incident which had caused him deep distress and pain and
had been weighing heavily on his mind. Hind was for-
given and the woman was stunned at this gentle generosity. Identifying herself she told the Prophet: 'Never
was a camp more hateful in my eyes than yours, and
today none is more beloved and beautiful than the camp
of the Apostle of God.'

Muhammad, in the hour of his triumph, restrained

his army from shedding blood and showed every sign of humility and thanksgiving. His resentment for treatment meted out to him in Mecca in the past might have excited him to revenge, but in fact the Apostle instructed his commanders that on entering Mecca they should only fight those who resisted, sparing women, children and old men. A number of persons, however, were to be killed even if they were found beneath the curtain of the Ka'ba.[28] Four men were put to death and among them were those who had apostatised. In comparison with acts of other conquerors, Muhammad's treatment of his enemies in Mecca is yet to be matched by a similar act of clemency anywhere in the world. Has any conqueror in history behaved so gently or mercifully with the vanquished foe?

CONCILIATING THE ANSAR AT HUNAYN

The Muslims are no longer the oppressed people that they were in Mecca. It is four years since the strongest citadel of the Quraysh fell, and the whole population of Mecca has accepted Islam—most of them presumably because it helps them ride on the crest of the rising tide, though there are certainly a very large number who have come with conviction. But whatever the motives, they are all accepted as Muslims and share as such all the benefits of a society based on essential equality. The armies of Islam are marching on—the bulk is now provided by the converts from Mecca. They are large in numbers but this does not necessarily lend strength to an army. Faith in Islam is the first factor, and this has not had time to work deeply on the minds of men who have just entered into its fold. This became obvious when the

Muslims, proud of their numbers, nearly lost the battle at Hunayn even though twelve thousand men were marching under the banner of Islam. The Prophet was literally left alone in the chaos of retreat. Without his supreme confidence and presence of mind the day might well have been lost. But where thousands wavered, one man stood alone and aloft and succeeded at last in rallying back his forces. The result was soon assured. No less than six thousand prisoners of war were captured besides twenty-four thousand camels, forty thousand sheep and heaps of silver and other material.

A deputation from Hunayn came to the Apostle in al-Ji'rana[29] where he held six thousand women and children and innumerable sheep and camels which had been captured from them. They begged him to have pity on them. 'The apostle said, "Which are dearest to you? Your sons and your wives or your cattle?" They replied, "Do you give us the choice between our cattle and our honour? Nay, give us back our wives and our sons, for that is what we most desire." He said, "So far as concerns what I and B. 'Abdu'l-Muttalib have they are yours. When I have prayed the noon prayers with the men then get up and say, 'We ask the apostle's intercession with the Muslims, and the Muslims' intercession with the apostle for our sons and wives.' I will then give them to you and make application on your behalf." When the apostle had ended the noon prayers they did as he had ordered them.'[30] The women and children of the Banu Hawazin were returned. Not only that; the Apostle asked the deputation to convey a message to Malik b. 'Auf, the haughty tribal chief of Ta'if, that if he came to him as a Muslim he would return his family and property and give him a hundred camels. On receiving the message the chief rode off to join the Apostle. 'He gave him back

his family and property and gave him a hundred camels.
He became an excellent Muslim and at the time he said:

"I have never seen or heard of a man
Like Muhammad in the whole world;
Faithful to his word, generous when asked for a gift,
And when you wish he will tell you of the future.
When the squadron shows its strength
When spears and swords that strike,
In the dust of war he is like a lion
Guarding its cubs in its den." '31

The Apostle returned the captives of Hunayn to their
people and rode away.

The booty was immense. The Prophet distributed
most of it to the newcomers from Mecca in preference
to the veterans from Medina—men who had helped him
when he was without visible support, who had given
him shelter when he was driven out from Mecca, who
had since fought valiantly in every battle and had not
held back anything from their leader. These men had
now been given a lesser share in the spoils of war. There
is a limit to loyalty, and whispers shake it more quickly
than arrows. Word went around that the Prophet hailed
after all from Mecca! During the period of stress he was
supported by the Ansar, but at the time of victory he
thought of his own kith and kin! The whispering campaign gathered momentum. Credulous ears appeared to
succumb to the suggestion. The development was capable
of devastating effects on the leadership of the Prophet
and the future of Islam. The Prophet reacted promptly
and sent for the disaffected Ansar. Addressing the Ansar
he said: 'Did I not come to you when you were erring and
God guided you? Did I not come to you when you were

poor and God made you rich? Did I not come to you
when you were enemies and God softened your hearts?'

As the Prophet posed each question with a style slow
and deliberate his audience sat still and silent. 'Why don't
you answer me, O Ansar?' he demanded. They said, 'How
shall we answer you? Kindness and generosity belong to
God and His Apostle.' 'No,' retorted the Prophet, 'had
you so wished you could have said with legitimate pride,
"Muhammad came to us discredited and we believed
in him; we gave him shelter and refuge when his own
kith and kin deserted him and drove him away; we
gave him help when he came to us a helpless man; we
took him in when he was a fugitive; we comforted him
when he was poor." Had you given me these answers
you would have spoken the truth. Are you now dis-
turbed,' he asked, 'because of the good things of this life
by which I win over a people that they may become
Muslims while I entrust Islam to you? Are you not satisfied that men should take away flocks and herds while
you take back with you the Apostle of God? By Him in
Whose hand is the soul of Muhammad, but for the migration I should be one of the Ansar myself. If all men went
one way and the Ansar another I should take the way of
the Ansar. God,' he prayed, 'have mercy on the Ansar,
their sons and their sons' sons!'

And thus ended the matter that might have led to a
mutiny! Many a grey beard in the audience was wet and
many a throat was choked with emotion. 'We are satisfied
with the Apostle of God as our lot and portion,' said the
Ansar. After the agitation had subsided, the Prophet
took pains to explain that his decision to show preference
to the Meccans was motivated by his anxiety to cement
their loyalty to Islam to which they had come only recently. The whole crisis was resolved, and there was not

a shadow of doubt lingering in any mind about the un-impeachable integrity of the Leader.

DEALINGS WITH THE HYPOCRITES

It was this weapon of tact and conciliation that averted many a crisis which threatened to destroy the inner unity of Islam in its early days. One can recall many an instance when a few words from the Prophet, spoken in the right manner at the right moment, helped resolve situations which might have developed into major crises from the slightest tactlessness in handling them. The student of Islamic history is aware, for example, of the deep sense of enmity which had existed for ages between the tribes of Aus and Khazraj in Medina. The irreconcilables were welded into the unity of lasting love by the patient and tactful handling of a leader who knew the value of peaceful negotiations. There was a time before the battle of Badr[32] when both the tribes were so poised against each other that the slightest provocation might have ended in their mutual destruction. It was on one of these explosive days that the Prophet happened to pass their way. Both Muslims and hypocrites were sitting together at one place. The former got up as the Prophet approached and offered all courtesies due to his station, while the latter, instead of offering salutations, came out with an impertinent remark. Here, then, was the much-dreaded spark! But the Prophet rose far above petty considerations of personal dignity and controlled the situation with a tactful remark. Three years later (A.H. 5) when a malicious lie was invented against 'A'yesha, the beloved wife of the Prophet, tempers ran so high that both the tribes were about to unsheath their swords right in the Prophet's own mosque, when Muhammad went up to the pulpit and changed the whole atmosphere of intense hostility into one of cordial love and brotherhood.

This happened immediately after his return from the expedition of Banu Musta'liq. Of the four-hundred-odd Muslims that comprised the force, many were hypocrites who had joined the expedition under their notorious leader 'Abdullah b. Ubayy—a man whom the Arabs had decided to crown king of Medina before Muhammad arrived there from Mecca. 'Abdullah b. Ubayy was an extremely influential man. He was intelligent and cunning, and having embraced Islam he tried hard to kill it from within. His was the role of an adroit saboteur in the garb of a follower. He was constantly on the lookout for opportunities to create dissensions. His was the function of an *agent provocateur,* dexterous in the ingenious methods he employed to further the unholy end he had in view. Surprisingly enough, his own son was a sincere and devoted Muslim and took part in none of the intrigues of the father against Islam. Both the son and the father happened to be together in the expedition which was now returning after a brief but successful encounter with a rebellious tribe. On their way back to Medina, the troops halted near a spring—the most attractive camping ground in a desert. A minor quarrel arose between a Muslim from Mecca and a Muslim from Medina while both had come to the spring to take their daily supply of water. The quarrel which was petty and personal soon assumed serious proportions. The whole camp was immediately divided into two hostile groups; those who belonged to Mecca unsheathed their swords to defend their own compatriots, and those who came from Medina were quick in taking up what was considered a challenge to their honour—a point on which blood could easily flow in Arabia for generations. The situation was tense. 'Abdullah b. Ubayy, the leader of the hypocrites, now assumed command of all Muslims from Medina because the whole quarrel centred around territorial and tribal loyalties. He added fuel to the fire by taunting Muslims from Medina saying that they had to blame nobody but themselves for their humiliating plight. He drove home the point that it was they who had invited the Muslims from Mecca, and these Muslims, having come to Medina to seek shelter, now had the audacity to consider themselves as equals and to challenge them to a fight! Nothing could be more humiliating than this and yet Muslims from Medina had nobody but themselves to blame for it! There was only one solution, he suggested, and that was to deny all help to the Meccans who would be thrown once again on their own in the vast wilderness of the desert without a home and without an ally!

This was a most inflammatory speech, and 'Abdullah b. Ubayy was determined to exploit the opportunity to the detriment of Islam. When news of this development reached the Prophet, 'Umar happened to be present in his camp. He was so furious and wild with rage that he entreated the Prophet for permission to kill the hypocrite who had so maliciously attempted to kill Islam. But Muhammad, though deeply pained at the news, was not moved by the passionate reaction of his close associate. 'Would you like it to be said,' he asked him, 'that Muhammad kills his own companions?' Instead he gave orders to set off. The men duly moved off. He travelled at a disagreeable time. The Apostle walked with the men all that day till nightfall, through the night until morning and during the following day until the sun became unbearable. Then he halted his men, and as soon as they touched the ground they fell asleep. He did this to distract their mind from what 'Abdullah b. Ubayy had said the day before.

He travelled through the Hijaz as far as Medina. The public mind had been set at rest. 'Abdullah b. Ubayy and his supporters had been kept guessing about the Prophet's reactions and the decision that he had taken in the matter. They naturally presumed that an extreme penalty was to be awarded for an extreme offence. It was widely rumoured that 'Abdullah b. Ubayy was to be executed for treason. His own son, having heard the rumour, rushed to the Prophet's camp. There he pleaded, not for mercy for his father who was a traitor to Islam, but for a concession to his own human weakness. If someone else was commissioned to put his father to the sword, argued the son, it was quite possible that he might be moved to avenge the death of his father. As a good Muslim he wanted to take no chances with his faith and he wished therefore to discharge the commission himself, if the Prophet had decided to execute his father. The son rose to the greatest heights of faith even as the father sank to the lowest depths of hypocrisy and treachery. The reward for this loyalty was prompt and generous. The Prophet assured him that he meant to punish the father by kindness and not by the sword. The result was that Ubayy's own people reproached and upbraided him roughly. The Apostle said to 'Umar when he heard of this state of things: 'Now, what do you think, 'Umar? Had I killed him on the day you wanted me to kill him, the leading men would have trembled with rage. If I ordered them to kill him today they would kill him.' 'Umar replied, 'I know that the Apostle's order is more blessed than mine.'[33] Later, when 'Abdullah b. Ubayy died a natural death, the Prophet led the funeral prayers notwithstanding all that he had done to sabotage the cause of Islam.

SLANDER ON 'A'YESHA[34]

'A'yesha was the most beloved wife of the Prophet. A young slim girl of fourteen years, she was the daughter of no less a person than his foremost follower and fastest friend, Abu Bakr. Whenever the Apostle decided to go on an expedition he would cast lots to decide which one of his wives should accompany him. On the occasion of the expedition to Banu Musta'liq (A.H. 5–6) the lot fell on 'A'yesha. It was an honour and a privilege to accompany the Prophet, and 'A'yesha was happy and excited. She borrowed a necklace from her sister Asma'. On the return journey the Prophet halted near Medina and passed a part of the night there. Then he gave orders to start early in the morning, and the men moved off. 'A'yesha at this time had gone out at some distance from the camp to ease herself. On returning to the camp she discovered that the borrowed necklace had slipped from her neck. The young girl rushed back in search of it, little knowing that the Prophet had ordered the march. She found the necklace but missed the caravan. The men who saddled her camel marched off with it in the belief that the lightweight passenger was on it. The men had gone when 'A'yesha reached the camp. There was no alternative but to wait. She wrapped herself in her smock and laid down there hoping that the men would come back for her when it was discovered that she was not on the camel. She had not waited long when Safwan b. al-Mu'attal, who manned the rearguard, appeared on the scene. It was his duty not to move with the caravan but to remain behind in order to ensure that anything left behind inadvertently was collected. Safwan was a companion of the Prophet. He had seen 'A'yesha before the veil was prescribed. He therefore easily recognised her even though she was wrapped up in her garments. He asked her what had kept her behind, but 'A'yesha did not speak to him. Then he brought up his camel and told 'A'yesha to ride it.

This was an ordinary incident which could occur in any journey. The hypocrites, however, made a malicious scandal out of it. Who would not react to such provocation when the chastity of a beloved wife is shamelessly assailed in public? The Prophet knew that 'Abdullah b. Ubayy was the author of this conspiracy. But all that he did was to mount the pulpit and say: 'O Muslims! who will procure me justice from the man who rails at my honour?' Trembling with rage, a companion got up to demand the name of the person who had invented the lie. The disclosure would have meant death to the man. The Prophet refused to divulge the name although he knew it well. He pacified the public and God soon cleared the honour of 'A'yesha. Even after this 'Abdullah b. Ubayy was not punished. The minor agents in the conspiracy were given the legal punishment, and they mended their ways after penitence. 'A'yesha was blissfully ignorant of the lie the hypocrites had invented against her. Since she fell seriously ill soon after her return to Medina and was taken to her mother, she heard nothing of what had happened. During her illness she missed the Apostle's usual kindness and attention to her but did not realise the reason for it; and it was not until she recovered, some twenty days later, that she learned of the matter. 'A'yesha received a terrible shock, and went back to her mother's house in a state of great commotion. She suffered agony till her conduct was cleared by the revelation. The Qur'an beautifully sums up the episode and points out the lesson that spotless purity in thought, word and deed includes the disposition to put the best construction on the motives of others, so that no evil motive should be

ascribed to the seeming indiscretion of a virtuous person.
Such a high standard can only come by the grace of God.

> Those who brought forward
> The lie are a body
> Among yourselves: think it not
> To be an evil to you;
> On the contrary it is good
> For you: to every man
> Among them (will come
> The punishment) of the sin
> That he earned, and to him
> Who took on himself the lead
> Among them, will be
> A Penalty grievous.
> Why did not the Believers—
> Men and women—when ye
> Heard of the affair,—put
> The best construction on it
> In their own minds
> And say, 'This (charge)
> Is an obvious lie'?
>
> Why did they not bring
> Four witnesses to prove it?
> When they have not brought
> The witnesses, such men,
> In the sight of God,
> (Stand forth) themselves as liars!
>
> Were it not for the grace
> And mercy of God on you,
> In this world and the Hereafter,
> A grievous penalty would have

Seized you in that ye rushed
Glibly into this affair.

Behold, you received it
On your tongues,
And said out of your mouths
Things of which ye had
No knowledge; and ye thought
It to be a light matter,
While it was most serious
In the sight of God.

And why did ye not,
When ye heard it, say?—
'It is not right of us
To speak of this:
Glory to God; this is
A most serious slander!'

God doth admonish you,
That ye may never repeat
Such (conduct), if ye
Are (true) Believers.
And God makes the Signs
Plain to you: for God
Is full of knowledge and wisdom.

Those who love (to see)
Scandal published broadcast
Among the Believers, will have
A grievous Penalty in this life
And in the Hereafter: God
Knows, and ye know not.

Were it not for the grace
And mercy of God on you,

And that God is
Full of kindness and mercy,
(Ye would be ruined indeed).[35]

One of the slanderers of 'A'yesha turned out to be a cousin of her father. The slanderer was in receipt of regular support in cash and kind from Abu Bakr who stopped this allowance after this incident and swore to support him no longer. But in accordance with the highest standards of Muslim ethics Abu Bakr could not be permitted to let personal resentment come in the way of helping a poor relation. This attitude would create resistance in the delinquent; tolerance and benevolence would help him mend his ways. The Qur'an exhorts a Muslim to forgive and overlook, for 'do you not want that God should forgive you and overlook your faults?'

And let not those who possess dignity and ease among you swear not to give to the near of kin and to the needy, and to fugitives for the cause of Allah. Let them forgive and show indulgence. Yearn ye not that Allah may forgive you? Allah is Forgiving, Merciful.[36]

CHAPTER

2

DELEGATIONS RECEIVED
AND DISPATCHED

I

DELEGATIONS RECEIVED
BY THE PROPHET

In the first year of the Islamic era (c.e. 622), Muhammad's aim was to gather more friends so that he and his followers could enjoy freedom of movement in their expeditions outside Medina and a safe and unmolested life in Medina itself. Having achieved this objective he started enlisting supporters to join him in the expeditions. To begin with, they came mainly from his sphere of influence in Medina. This was part of his program of consolidating his own strength and building a complex of tribes in alliance with himself. The aim of winning the Meccans for Islam was realised later, but even by the time of the Pact of Hudaybiya (which was made nearly two years before the conquest of Mecca) there was little doubt about the political importance of the Prophet in the life of Arabia.

In following the course of Muhammad's 'diplomacy,' however, we should clearly understand that clans in contemporary Arabia acted as sovereign bodies and made alliances with other clans as equals, and not subordinate to any one of them. Muhammad, in the Medina years, was by no means the undisputed ruler of Arabia; in fact, he was merely one of the important men, and there were others who were far more influential. The tribe was an important fact. The divisions and the subdivisions were not mere nomenclatures but a political reality to be reckoned with. Within each group there were smaller groups intensely jealous of one another. When we hear of a deputation from a tribe being received by Muhammad, it should not be taken to mean that the entire tribe was represented. On the contrary, it was often only a faction. Here lay the effectiveness of Muhammad as a negotiator, for in the contrary and contradictory affiliations of the tribes his success depended on his extensive knowledge of the internal politics of each group and the wisdom in deciding which faction to receive, support and negotiate with. We should remember the fact that in dealing with the tribes, Muhammad was handling a most complex situation which became all the more difficult because his method was that of persuasion and patience.

In describing the deputations received by the Prophet and the embassies sent out by him we have used the analytic method to bring out the importance of various events, but Muhammad, it must be remembered, thought intuitively and not analytically. He was, of course, aware of all the factors we have enumerated but, without isolating these in his thinking, he was able to decide on a course of action that was an adequate response to them. His is naturally the approach of an inspired prophet rather than that of a tactician, strategist or logician.

Muhammad received a large number of deputations in the ninth year of the Hijra (April 630–March 631). He now had the supreme authority in Arabia. Mecca had been conquered. It was the Quraysh who had waged war against him. Now that they had given in, the rest of

Arabia followed, for the Quraysh were the leaders of Arabia, the people of the Sacred Temple, the pure stock of Isma'il, son of Abraham, and if they could not resist Muhammad, the rest of the tribes knew that they could not continue to fight him.

We will briefly cover some of the deputations which the Apostle received the whole year round in order to bring out the atmosphere in the capital of the new state headed by the Prophet. A few words about the position of the head of state and the privileges enjoyed by envoys would be relevant before we proceed with a detailed study of the embassies received by the Prophet. In Islam the head of state does not enjoy complete immunity such as some modern systems of law seem to confer by declaring that the king can do no wrong. He is liable, like any other citizen, to be tried in an ordinary court for flouting the law. The Prophet is on record as having heard cases against his own person.[1] In the closing days of his life he thus addressed a public gathering: 'People! you may have had claims against me. If I have whipped anybody's back, let him retaliate on this my back. If I have condemned or censured anybody's honour, here is my honour to take revenge upon. If I have taken anybody's property, here is my property; let him take it. . . . In fact dearest to me is the one who takes his claim from me if he has a right thereto, or forgives me. Thus I shall meet my Lord with a clear conscience.' A man rose and claimed that the Prophet had borrowed some money from him. This was at once paid to him.[2] The Prophet established that the ruler is as much subject to law as an ordinary citizen of a state.

Generous treatment was, however, accorded to envoys. Together with their staff they enjoyed full personal immunity. They were not to be killed or in any way molested or maltreated.[3] Even if the envoy or any of his company was a criminal convicted by the state to which he was accredited, he was not to be treated otherwise than as an envoy. Envoys were accorded full freedom of prayer and religious rites. The Prophet allowed the delegation of the Christians of Najran to hold their service in his mosque. Only in extraordinary cases were envoys to be detained or imprisoned. The Prophet detained the plenipotentiaries of Mecca until the Muslim envoy detained by the Quraysh in Mecca returned safe to Hudaybiya.[4]

The Quraysh sent Abu Ra'fi as an envoy to negotiate peace with the Muslims. He was received by the Prophet. The ambassador who had come to represent the enemy declared his faith in Islam and refused to return. The Prophet admonished him: 'You are an ambassador. You must therefore go back, and if you still feel as strongly about Islam as you do now, you are always at liberty to return as a common Muslim.'

This view was taken by the Prophet at a time in Arabia when the person of an ambassador was not treated as inviolable in practice. We have earlier had an opportunity of seeing how the Prophet's own envoy was detained by the Quraysh during the negotiations of Hudaybiya and how his camel was killed, and all this happened years after Badr. It was the Prophet who set up the much-needed precedent, and he stuck to it all through, thus creating a healthy atmosphere for diplomacy to thrive in a land which was given to feuds and bloodshed and which realised but little the value of the art of negotiation in human relations. There is an incident on record that the envoy of Musaylima—the man who was later to lay a false claim to prophethood—was extremely rude and provocative in his behaviour towards the Prophet, but the Prophet, though gravely hurt, allowed no deviation. The envoy continued to enjoy immunity. This

diplomatic privilege was accorded to all envoys by the
Prophet. He did not insist on his prior consent before
a tribe or a country could send him an emissary acceptable to him. There is the interesting case of Wahshi,
the Abyssinian who had barbarously murdered Hamza,
the uncle of the Prophet, in the battle of Uhud. He was
mortally afraid to accept the assignment, but the enemies
of Islam themselves assured him that the Prophet did not
ever touch the person of an envoy. And so was it proved
when Wahshi presented his credentials. The treatment
he received was both unexpected and unparalleled in the
annals of Arab history, and it was because of this that
Wahshi, among several other envoys, embraced Islam.
It was the Prophet's scrupulous adherence to his promises,
his reputation for keeping faith under all circumstances,
and his ability fully to guard the trust reposed in him
that inspired confidence even in his inveterate enemies.

The Prophet when in Medina received delegations
and embassies in his mosque, where the Pillar of Embassies still commemorates the institution. Before envoys
had an audience with the Prophet, they were instructed
by some sort of master of ceremonies in local formalities
which they sometimes disregarded.[5] The Prophet and
his companions usually put on fine dresses at the time of
the ceremonial reception of envoys who generally presented and received gifts. The gifts received by the
Prophet went to the state treasury.[6] If a Muslim envoy
received a gift from a foreign ruler, it also went to the
state coffers.[7] The envoys were officially entertained.
There were several large houses in Medina in the time
of the Prophet, specially meant for foreign guests. The
treatment accorded the envoys corresponded to their
personal status and position and the ranks of those whom
they represented.

Deputation from Ta'if

The people of Ta'if were next only to the pagans of Mecca in their persecution of the Prophet. It was in the streets of Ta'if that he was tortured to the point of bleeding. Even after the major part of Arabia had come under the sway of the Prophet, Ta'if stood apart in scornful defiance until it could no longer ignore the *de facto* supremacy of Islam. In fact it was the last to submit and it was not until A.H. 9, a couple of years before the Prophet's death, that a deputation from Ta'if went to Medina to declare their submission. The Prophet personally received the leader of the delegation and, although this envoy was not a Muslim, his tents were pitched in the premises of the Prophet's mosque—the highest honour which could be conferred on a guest. This gave the visitors an opportunity to witness for themselves the devotion and the spirit of brotherhood obtaining among the Muslims. With all their hostility and hatred of Islam, the delegation declared after some time their willingness to accept it with certain conditions which they considered quite reasonable. In fact, they had thought that the Muslims would gladly welcome them to their ranks, for the conversion of Ta'if would indeed bring immense strength and prestige to Islam. Their assumption was not far wrong, but having no moral scruples themselves, they had perhaps counted on the Prophet to barter away his principles for big political gains. With some such consideration at the back of their minds, the delegation from Ta'if offered to accept Islam on the following conditions:

(a) Adultery shall be permitted to the people of Ta'if. This, they explained, was essential because most of them in their society remained bachelors and had to resort to this means of satisfying their animal passions.

(b) Usury shall be permitted. This, it was argued, was again essential because interest was the fundamental basis of their economic life which could not flourish if the Qur'anic injunctions against interest were to apply to them.

(c) Drinking of liquor shall be allowed. This concession was demanded because Ta'if produced a large quantity of grapes and prohibition would ruin their trade.

The negotiations continued for some time, and after the delegation was convinced that these concessions could not possibly be granted without seriously undermining the tenets of Islam, the demands were withdrawn in favour of the following fresh proposals:

(a) That the people of Ta'if shall not be called upon to break the idol of al-Lat—their greatest god—for three years.

(b) That they shall be exempted from following the Qur'anic injunction about *Prayers, Zakat* and *Jihad.*

Anyone with even a cursory acquaintance with the principles of Islam will readily concede that no negotiations could have been possible on the basis of these demands. The conditions were ridiculous and offered no common ground for discussion. Yet the Prophet patiently continued the negotiations and ultimately found a formula which satisfied the parties concerned. A compromise was reached on the first demand. It was agreed that the people of Ta'if who had worshipped the idol of al-Lat for centuries would be spared the agony of breaking it to pieces. This task was therefore to be undertaken by a Muslim to be deputed by the Prophet. This proved a workable compromise, acceptable to both parties.

The second demand was more difficult to negotiate. The Prophet found himself unable to accord exemption from prayers, a duty a Muslim has to discharge five times a day. Zakat is leviable but once in a year and the obligation of Jihad arises only when conditions demand it. It was agreed, therefore, that while no exemption would be accorded from the observance of daily prayers, exemption would, however, be granted from the payment of Zakat and participation in Jihad. The Prophet appears to have offered a compromise on the basic tenets of Islam. But what was the result? Within two years of the negotiation of this agreement we see not a soul in Ta'if wishing even remotely to violate the discipline of Islam. Having assimilated the spirit of the new faith and having learned to pray five times a day, their conduct was regulated by their religion which inspired in them consciousness of higher values of life. The apparent discord between the religious and the economic interests implied in the concessions was transcended in their growing sense of an integrated personality which emerged after the acceptance of Islam by the people of Ta'if. This, then, was not a compromise. It only appears to be so. On the contrary, it provides evidence of the Prophet's rich and keen insight into human nature.

The episode is a striking illustration of the value of tact, compromise and judgment in the conduct of negotiations. A man with lesser gifts would have broken off the negotiations before they had started, for to an ordinary man there hardly appears to have been any ground for starting the talks at all!

Deputation from the Christians of Najran

This deputation[8] comprised sixty members, three of whom were in control of affairs: namely, the *'Aqib,* the leader of the people who took policy decisions, the *Sayyid,* an administrator in charge of transport and general arrangements, and finally the *Usquf* (bishop) who was a scholar and religious leader. Abu Harith, the bishop in the delegation, was a great scholar who was known for his knowledge and zeal for religion. The Christian kings of Byzantium had lavished honours on him for his scholarship and he was recognised by his contemporaries as an authority in this field.

The delegation came to Medina and entered the Apostle's mosque as he was saying the afternoon prayers. They were elegantly clad in Yamani garments, cloaks and mantles. The time of their prayers having come, they stood and prayed towards the east in the Apostle's mosque. They were allowed to do so. The Prophet is stated to have told them: 'Conduct your service here in the mosque. It is a place consecrated to God.' All the members of the deputation were Byzantine Christians.

A discussion took place about the Apostle's view of Christianity, the main point of controversy being the Christian belief in the divinity of Christ. The Prophet read more than eighty verses from the Sura of the Family of 'Imran. Those who are conversant with the Qur'an know the line of argument running through these verses: There is no associate of God in His authority. Jesus was one who was formed in the womb like all other children of Adam; how can he be a God when he springs from the womb? God gave power to Jesus in matters of virtue such as raising the dead, healing the sick, enlivening birds of clay, and declaring the unseen; He withheld from him such powers as the appointment of kings by a prophetic command, making the night pass into day and the day into night. . . . If they had an example and a clear proof that he were a god, all that would be within his power, while they know that he fled from kings and because of them moved from country to country. And then there is mentioned in great detail how the virgin conceived in her purity. God 'created Adam from earth by that same power without a male or a female. And he was as Jesus was: flesh and blood and hair and skin. The creation of Jesus without a male is no more wonderful than this. "Whoso argues with thee about him after knowledge has come to thee. . . . Then say: Come, let us summon our sons and your sons, our wives and your wives, ourselves and yourselves, then let us pray earnestly and invoke God's curse upon the liars. Verily this . . . is the true story. . . . There is no God but God and God is Mighty Wise. If they turn back God knows about the corrupt doers. Say, O Scripture folk, Come to a just word between us that we will worship only God and associate nothing with Him and some of us will not take others as lords beside God. And if they turn back say: Bear witness that we are Muslims" ' [iii. 61–64].[9]

The Prophet, after having finished the argument in the light of the Qur'an, invited the Christians to justice and, if they opposed him in the view expressed on Christ, to a mutual invocation of a curse.

There were consultations among the deputation. The 'Aqib, the chief adviser, is stated to have said:

"You know right well that Muhammad is a Prophet . . . and he has brought a decisive declaration about the nature of your master. You know too that a people has never invoked a curse on a Prophet and seen its elders live and its youth grow up. If you do this you will be exterminated. But if you decide to adhere to your religion and to maintain your doctrine about your master, then take your leave of the man and go home." So they came to the apostle and told him that they had decided not to resort to cursing . . . and return home.[10]

They, however, made a request for a man who might be able to decide certain financial matters in dispute among them. The Apostle sent for Abu 'Ubayda b. al-

Jarrah, a firm and trusted man, and told him to 'go with them and judge between them faithfully in matters they dispute about.'[11]

Deputation from Banu Sa'd

Among the deputations was one from Banu Sa'd. The leader was Dimam b. Tha'labah. When he came

he made his camel kneel at the gate of the mosque, hobbled it, and went into the mosque where the apostle was sitting with his companions. Now Dimam was a thickset hairy man with two forelocks. He came forward until he stood over the apostle and said, "Which of you is the son of 'Abdu'l-Muttalib? . . . I am going to ask you a hard question, so don't take it amiss." The apostle told him to ask what he liked . . . he said, "I adjure you by God your God and the God of those before you and the God of those who will come after you, has God sent you to us as an apostle?" "Yes, by God He has," he replied. He then adjured him to answer the questions: "Has He ordered you to order us to serve Him alone and not associate anything with Him and to discard those rival deities which our fathers used to worship along with Him; and to pray these five prayers; then the ordinances of Islam one by one, alms, fasting, pilgrimage and all the laws of Islam?" At the end he said, "I testify that there is no God but Allah and I testify that Muhammad is the apostle of God, and I will carry out these ordinances, and I will avoid what you have forbidden me to do; I will neither add to, nor diminish from them."

The man went to his camel, freed it from its hobble, and went off to his people, and when they gathered to him the first thing he said was, "How evil are al-Lat and al-'Uzza!" "Heavens above, Dimam," they said, "beware of leprosy and elephantiasis and madness!" He said: "Woe to you, they (idols) can neither hurt nor heal. God has sent an apostle and sent down to him a book, so seek deliverance thereby from your present state; as for me, I bear witness that there is no God but the one God who is without associate, and that Muhammad is His slave and apostle."[12]

Deputation from Banu Tayyi'

The deputation from Tayyi'—the tribe proverbial for its generosity—came among others. 'Adiy b. Hatim, the leader of the tribe who was extremely hostile to the Apostle, used to say,

No Arab disliked the apostle when he first heard of him more than I. Now I was a chief of noble birth, a Christian, and I used to travel about among my people to collect a quarter of their stock. I was my own master in religious matters and was a king among my people and treated as such. When I heard of the apostle I disliked him and said to an Arab servant of mine who was looking after my camels, "Prepare some of my well-trained, well-fed camels, and keep them near me, and when you hear of Muhammad's army coming into this country bring me word." One morning he came to me and said, "Whatever you are going to do when Muhammad's cavalry comes upon you, do it now, for I have seen flags and I learn that they are the troops of Muhammad." I ordered him to bring my camels and I put my family and children on them and decided to join my fellow Christians in Syria. I went as far as al-Jaushiya and I left one of Hatim's daughters in the settlement. When I reached Syria I stopped there.

In my absence the apostle's cavalry came and among the captives they took was Hatim's daughter, and she was brought to the apostle among the captives of Tayyi'. The apostle had heard of my flight to Syria. Hatim's daughter was put in the enclosure by the door of the mosque in which the captives were imprisoned, and the apostle passed by her. She got up to meet him, for she was a courteous woman, and said, "O apostle of God, my father is dead, and the man who should act for me has gone. If you spare me God will spare you." He asked her who her man was and when she told him it was 'Adiy b. Hatim he exclaimed, "The man who runs away from God and His apostle." Then he went on and left her. Exactly the same thing happened the next day, and on the following day she was in despair. Then a man behind her motioned her to get up and speak to him. She said the same words as before and he replied, "I have done so, but do not hurry away until you find one of your people whom you can trust who can take you to your country, then let me know." . . . [Hatim's daughter said] "The apostle gave me clothing and put me on a camel and gave me money and I went away until I came to Syria."

'Adiy said: "I was sitting among my people when I saw a howdah making for us and I said, 'It is Hatim's daughter' and so it was, and when she got to me she reviled me, saying, 'You evil rascal, you carried away your family and children and abandoned your father's daughter.' I said, 'Do not say anything that is bad, little sister, for by God I have no excuse. I did do what you say.' Then she alighted and stayed with me; and as she was a discreet woman I asked her what she thought of this man and she said, 'I think that you should join him quickly, for if the man is a prophet then those who get to him first will be preferred; and if he is a king you will not be shamed in the glory of al-Yaman, you being the man you are.' I said that this was a sound judgement so I went to the apostle when he was in his mosque in Medina and saluted him and told him my name and he got up to take me to his house. As we were making for it there met him an old feeble woman who asked him to stop and he stopped for a long time while she told him of her needs. I said to myself, 'This is no king.' Then he took me into his house and took hold of a leather cushion stuffed with palm leaves and threw it to me saying, 'Sit on that.' I said, 'No, you sit on it,' and he said, 'No, you.' So I sat on it and he sat on the ground. I said to myself, 'This is not the way a king behaves.' . . . Then he said, 'It may well be that the poverty you see prevents you from joining this religion but, by God, wealth will soon flow so copiously among them that there will not be the people to take it. But perhaps it is that you see how many are their enemies and how few they are? But, by God, you will hear of a woman coming on her camel from Qadisiya to visit this temple unafraid. But perhaps it is that you see that others have the power and sovereignty, but by God you will soon hear that the white castles of Babylon have been opened to them.' "[13]

'Adiy became a Muslim. The two things happened during his lifetime; the third happened soon after.

Deputation from Banu Tamim

When the deputation from Banu Tamim entered the mosque, the Prophet was in his house. They shouted for him, 'Come out to us, Muhammad, we have come to compete with you in boasting, so give permission to our poet and our orator.' The vulgar manner of address and the challenge to frivolous boasting annoyed the Prophet, but he came out to receive them; he gave no expression to his annoyance but settled down to negotiate with them in the manner that they understood.

Diplomacy by oratory was not unknown to the Greeks; the Arabs added the element of poetry to it. 'Utarid b. Hajib, the orator of Banu Tamim, on getting permission from the Apostle to state his case, got up and said:

Praise belongs to God for His favour to us and He is worthy to be praised, who has made us kings and given us great wealth wherewith we are generous, and has made us the strongest people of the east and the greatest in number, and the best equipped, so who among mankind is our equal? Are we not the princes of men and their superiors? He who would compete with us let him enumerate what we have enumerated. If we wished we could say more, but we are too modest to say much of what He has given us and are well known for that. I say this that you may bring forward the like and anything better.[14]

The Muslim orator, Thabit b. Qays, then got up to speak thus:

Praise belongs to God Who created heaven and earth and established His rule therein, and His knowledge includes His throne; nothing exists but by His bounty. By His power He made us kings and chose the best of his creation as an apostle, and honoured him with lineage, made him truthful in speech, and favoured him with reputation, and sent down to him His book and entrusted him with it above (all) that He had created. He was God's choice from the worlds. Then He summoned men to believe in him, and the emigrants from his people and his kinsmen believed in God's apostle; the most noble men in reputation, the highest in dignity, and the best in deeds. The first of creatures to answer and respond to God when the apostle called them were ourselves. We are God's helpers and the assistants of His apostle, and will fight men until they believe in God; and he who believes in God and His apostle has protected his life and property from us; and he who disbelieves we will fight in God unceasingly. . . . These are my words and I ask God's pardon for myself and the believers both men and women. Peace upon you.[15]

After the speeches were over—the radical difference of approach of the Jahiliyya and Islam is obvious in the two orations—the poets came into the arena. Al-Zibriqan, the poet of Banu Tamim, said:

We are the nobles, no tribe can equal us.
From us kings are born and in our midst churches are
 built.
How many tribes have we plundered,
For excellence in glory is to be sought after.
In time of dearth we feed our meat to the hungry
When no rain-cloud can be seen.
You can see chiefs coming to us from every land,
And we feed them lavishly.
We slaughter fat-humped young camels as a matter of
 course,
Guests when they come are satisfied with food.
You will see whenever we challenge a tribe's
 superiority
They yield and abandon leadership.
He who challenges us knows the result:
His people withdraw and the news is noised abroad.
We forbid others but none forbid us.
Thus we are justly exalted in pride.[16]

The Muslim poet, Hassan b. Qays, then rose and
recited:

The leaders of Fihr and their brothers
Have shown a way of life to be followed.
Everyone whose heart is devout
And does all manner of good approves them.
Such a people when they fight injure their enemies
Or gain the advantage of their adherents which they seek.
Such is their nature—no recent habit.
(The worst of characteristics is innovation.)
If there are men who surpass those who come after them
Then they would be behind the last of them.
Men do not repair what their hands have destroyed in
 fighting,

Nor destroy what they have repaired.
If they compete with others they take the lead.
If weighed against men famous for liberality they send
    down the scale.
Chaste men whose chastity is mentioned in revelation,
Undefiled, no impurity can injure them.
Not mean with their wealth towards the sojourner
And no stain of covetousness touches them.
When we attack a tribe we do not go softly to them
Like a calf running to the wild cow.
We rise up when the claws of war reach us
When good-for-naughts are humbled by its nails.
They do not boast when they overcome their enemy,
And if they are beaten they are not weak nor despairing.
In battle when death is at hand
They are like lions in Halya with crooked claws.
Take what you can get if they are enraged
And seek not what they have forbidden.
To fight them is to meet poison and bane
So do not antagonize them.
How noble the people who have God's apostle with them
When sects and parties differ!
My heart sings their praises
Aided in its beloved task by an eloquent and ready
    tongue,
For they are the best of all creatures
In matters grave and gay.[17]

The deputation from the Banu Tamim is representative of the frivolous tribal approach of the Jahiliyya to Islam. But however frivolous the approach, the Prophet made an earnest attempt at explaining to them the concept of Islam in a simple straightforward manner. Another man in his place would not have agreed to receive such frivolous men, but the Prophet not only received them with kindness and courtesy but also decided to negotiate with them in the manner that was peculiarly their own.

Deputation from Banu Hanifa

In the deputation from Banu Hanifa was Musaylima b. Habib, al-Kazzab, i.e. the arch liar. The deputation came to the Apostle

having left Musaylima behind with the camels and the baggage. When they had accepted Islam they remembered where he was, and told the apostle that they had left a companion of theirs to guard their stuff. The apostle ordered that he should be given the same [presents] as the rest, saying, "His position is no worse than yours," i.e. in minding the property of his companions. . . . Then they left the apostle and brought him what he had given him. When they reached al-Yamama the enemy of God [Musaylima] apostatized, gave himself out as a prophet, and played the liar. He said, "I am a partner with him in the affair," and then he said to the deputation . . . "Did he not say to you when you mentioned me to him, 'His position is no worse than yours'? What can that mean but that he knows that I am a partner with him in the affair?" Then he began to speak . . . in imitation of the style of the Quran . . . He permitted them to drink wine and fornicate, and let them dispense with prayer, yet he was acknowledging the apostle as a prophet.[18]

Later Musaylima sent two messengers with a letter from him to the Apostle. The letter said: 'From Musaylima the apostle of God to Muhammad the apostle of God. Peace upon you. I have been made partner with you in authority. To us belongs half the land and to Quraysh half, but Quraysh are a hostile people.'[19] When the Apostle read the letter he asked the two messengers who had brought it whether they agreed with the contents. They said they held the same views as Musaylima. The Apostle 'replied, "By God, were it not that heralds are not to be killed I would behead the pair of you!" Then he wrote to Musaylima: "From Muhammad the apostle of God to Musaylima the liar. Peace be upon him who follows the guidance. The earth is God's. He lets whom He will of His creatures inherit it and the result is to the pious." This was at the end of the year 10.'[20]

Kings of Himyar[21]

The Prophet received a messenger from the kings of Himyar with their acceptance of Islam and abandonment of polytheism and its adherents. He wrote to them:

In the name of God the Compassionate, the Merciful, from Muhammad the apostle of God, the prophet, to al-Harith b. 'Abdu Kulal and to Nu'aym b. 'Abdu Kulal and to al-Nu'man prince of Dhu Ru'ayn and Ma'afir and Hamdan. I praise God the only God unto you. Your messenger reached me on my return from the land of the Byzantines and he met us in Medina and conveyed your message and your news and informed us of your Islam. . . . God has guided you with His guidance. If you do well and obey God and His apostle and perform prayer, and pay alms, and God's fifth [khums] of booty and the apostle's share and selected part, and the poor tax which is incumbent on believers from land. . . . This is what God has laid upon the believers. Anyone who does more it is to his merit. He who fulfils this and bears witness to his Islam and helps the believers against the polytheists he is a believer with a believer's rights and obligations and he has the guarantee of God and His apostle. If a Jew or a

Christian becomes a Muslim he is a believer with his rights and obligations. He who holds fast to his religion, Jew or Christian, is not to be turned from it. He must pay the poll tax [*jizya*]—for every adult, male or female, free or slave, one full dinar . . . or its equivalent in clothes. He who pays that to God's apostle has the guarantee of God and His apostle, and he who withholds it is the enemy of God and His apostle.

The apostle of God, Muhammad the prophet, has sent to Zur'a Dhu Yazan: When my messengers Mu'adh b. Jabal, and 'Abdullah b. Zayd, and Malik b. 'Ubada . . . and their companions come to you I commend them to your good offices. Collect the alms and the poll tax from your provinces and hand them over to my messengers. . . . Muhammad witnesses that there is no God but Allah and that he is His servant and apostle.

Malik b. Murra al-Rahawi has told me that you were the first of Himyar to accept Islam . . . and I congratulate you and order you to treat Himyar well and not to be false and treacherous, for the apostle of God is the friend both of your poor and your rich. The alms tax [Zakat] is not lawful to Muhammad or his household; it is alms to be given to the poor Muslims and the [poor] wayfarer [*ibn al-sabil*]. Malik has brought the news and kept secret what is confidential, and I order you to treat him well. I have sent to you some of the best of my people, religious and learned men, and I order you to treat them well, for they must be respected. Peace upon you and the mercy and blessings of God.[22]

Deputation of Kinda[23]

The deputation of Kinda came to the mosque with eighty riders. They had combed their locks and blackened their eyes with *kuhl*, and they wore striped robes bordered with silk. The Apostle asked them if they had

accepted Islam, and when they said that they had, he
asked why this silk was on their bodies. They tore it off
and threw it away!

II

DELEGATIONS DISPATCHED BY THE
PROPHET

The First Embassy of Islam: Mission to the Negus

While the Prophet received deputations from various
tribes in Arabia, and envoys from various neighbouring
rulers, he also sent envoys to the Arab and non-Arab
rulers in the period between al-Hudaybiya and his death
on 8 June 632. The first Muslim mission went to Abyssinia in the early Meccan period when the Prophet and
his followers were subjected to extreme persecution by
the Quraysh. A batch of Muslims left for Abyssinia with
the permission of the Prophet and succeeded in securing
the protection of the Negus. The Quraysh could not bear
to see any Muslim safely ensconced in the protection of
the Negus. They sent a strong delegation to persuade the
king to give them up. Many valuable presents were sent;
the generals were heavily bribed to intercede with the
king on behalf of the Arab delegation. The Negus, however, refused to surrender the Muslim refugees without
hearing their case. Ja'far b. Abu Talib spoke for the
Muslims when the king asked for reasons which had led
to the flight from their homeland. 'O King,' he said,

> we were an uncivilized people, worshipping idols, eating
> corpses, committing abominations, breaking natural ties,
> . . . and our strong devoured our weak. Thus we were
> until God sent unto us an apostle whose lineage, truth,

trustworthiness and clemency we know. He summoned us to acknowledge God's unity and to worship Him and to renounce the stones and images which we and our fathers formerly worshipped. He commanded us to speak the truth, be faithful to our engagements, mindful of the ties of kinship and kindly hospitality, and to refrain from crimes and bloodshed. He forbade us to commit abominations and to speak lies, and to devour the property of orphans, to vilify chaste women. He commanded us to worship God alone and not to associate anything with Him, and he gave us orders about prayers, giving of alms and fasting. . . . We confessed his truth and believed in him, and we followed him in what he had brought from God, and we worshipped God alone without associating aught with Him. We treated as forbidden what he forbade, and as lawful what he declared lawful. Thereupon our people attacked us, treated us harshly and seduced us from our faith to try to make us go back to the worship of idols instead of the worship of God, and to regard as commendable the evil deeds we once committed. So when they got the better of us, treated us unjustly, circumscribed our lives, and came between us and our religion, we came to your country, having chosen you above all others. Here we have been happy in your protection, and we hope that we shall not be treated unjustly while we are with you.[24]

Ja'far then recited a passage from the Qur'an.

The plan of the Quraysh was frustrated. The Negus refused to surrender the Muslims. The Quraysh did not, however, give in. They laid a trap for the next day. They thought of provoking the Negus by telling him that the Muslims did not believe in the divinity of Jesus, son of Mary. When a question was put to Ja'far in this regard he said, 'We say about him that which our Prophet brought, that Jesus is the servant of God, and His apostle, and His spirit, and His word, which He cast into

Mary the virgin.' The generals of the Negus snorted when he said this but the king's reaction was different. He took a straw from the ground and said, 'By God, Jesus, son of Mary, does not exceed what you have said by the length of this straw.' The Muslims were safe. The Quraysh were humiliated. Their presents were returned. They left the Negus crestfallen, taking away their presents while the Muslims lived with him in peace and security.

Meanwhile in Mecca 'Umar had accepted Islam. This was an accession of strength. The Apostle's companions who had gone to Abyssinia heard that the Meccans had accepted Islam, and they set out for the homeland. On nearing Mecca they discovered that the report was false. They entered Mecca by stealth, perhaps under the protection of some citizen. The conduct of Muslims in Abyssinia did not fail to impress the Christians there. The Prophet received a deputation of some twenty Christians in Mecca. They were received in the Ka'ba. When they had asked all the questions, they were so satisfied with the answers that they accepted Islam. When they got up to go away, Abu Jahl with a number of Quraysh intercepted them, saying, 'God, what a wretched band you are! Your people at home sent you to bring them information about the fellow, and as soon as you sat with him you renounced your religion and believed what he said. We don't know a more asinine band than you.' They answered, 'Peace be upon you. We will not engage in foolish controversy with you. We have our religion and you have yours. We have not been remiss in seeking what is best.'

We have mentioned the mission of Ja'far b. Abu Talib to the court of Abyssinia where some Muslims took refuge before the emigration to Medina. Ja'far carried a letter from the Apostle for the Negus. It said:

From Muhammad the apostle of God to the Negus al-Asham king of Abyssinia, Peace. I praise Allah unto you the King, the Holy, the Peace, the Faithful, the Watcher, and I bear witness that Jesus son of Mary is the spirit of God and His word which He cast to Mary the Virgin, the good, the pure, so that she conceived Jesus. God created him from His spirit and His breathing as He created Adam by His hand and His breathing. I call you to God the Unique without partner and to His obedience, and to follow me and to believe in that which came to me, for I am the apostle of God. I have sent to you my nephew Ja'far with a number of Muslims, and when they come to you entertain them without haughtiness, for I invite you and your armies to God. I have accomplished (my work) and my admonitions, so receive my advice. Peace upon all those that follow true guidance![25]

Instructions to Envoys

The spirit of sympathy, tact and judgment governed the Prophet's standing instructions to his envoys who were accredited to numerous cities, communities and countries to convey his message. Their directions were to work with patience and avoid severity, to give good tidings to the people and not to incite hostility towards their mission. In the case of people with some kind of religion, the envoys had orders to invite their attention to the unity of God and to persuade them to have faith in all the prophets of God in the first instance. If they accepted the basic minimum, they were to be told that God had ordained prayers five times a day; and if they accepted this obligation too, they were then to be told that the rich among them owed Zakat to the poor. The money was to be collected and spent in the same locality or society so that the people had a chance to witness for themselves the benefit of this injunction. While this would confirm the poor in their faith, the rich were not to be treated harshly and the envoys were told not to select the best of their possessions in payment of Zakat. Consideration was to be shown to all alike and no injustice was to be done under any circumstances.

In A.H. 10 Khalid b. al-Walid, the famous general, came to Medina with a deputation from Banu al-Harith. They had accepted Islam before they came to the Prophet. The deputation returned after having met the Prophet who appointed 'Amr b. Hazm to instruct them in Islam. In a letter to him the Prophet sets out a directive which lays down the basic principles of moral conduct to be observed by an adherent of Islam.

This is a clear announcement from God and His apostle. O you who believe, be faithful to your agreements. The instructions of Muhammad the prophet the apostle of God to 'Amr b. Hazm when he sent him to the Yaman. He orders him to observe piety in all his doings for God is with those who are pious and who do well; and he commanded him to behave with truth as God commanded him; and that he should give people the good news and command them to follow it and to teach men the Quran and instruct them in it and to forbid men to do wrong so that none but the pure should touch the Quran and should instruct men in their privileges and obligations and be lenient to them when they behave aright and severe on injustice, for God hates injustice and has forbidden it . . . and if there is a quarrel between men forbid them to appeal to tribes and families, and let their appeal be to God; they who do not appeal to God but to tribes and families let them be smitten with the sword until their appeal is made to God; and command men to perform the ablutions, [to wash] their faces, and their hands to the elbows and their feet to the ankles, and let them wipe [wash] their heads as God has ordered; and command prayer at the proper time with bowing, prostration and humble reverence; prayers at daybreak, at noon when the sun declines, in the afternoon when the sun is descending, at even when the night approaches not delaying it until the stars appear in the sky; later at the beginning of the night; order them to run to the mosques when they are summoned, and to wash when they go to them, and order them to take from the booty God's fifth and what alms are enjoined on the Muslims from land—a tithe of what the fountains water and the sky waters, and a twentieth of what the bucket waters; and for every ten camels two sheep; and for every twenty camels four sheep, for every forty cows one cow; for every thirty cows a bull or cow calf; for every forty sheep at grass one sheep; this is what God has enjoined on the believers in the matter of alms. He who adds thereto it is a merit to him. A Jew or a Christian who becomes a sincere Muslim of his own accord and obeys the religion of Islam is a believer with the same rights and the same obligations. If one of them holds fast to his religion he is not to be turned from it. Every adult, male or female, bond or free, must pay a golden dinar or its equivalent in clothes. He who performs this has the guarantee of God and His apostle; he who withholds it is the enemy of God and His apostle and all believers.[26]

It will be seen that truth in itself is not enough to succeed. It must be communicated with patience, tact and calm. The process should be slow and gradual and no spectacular results should be expected overnight even from a revealed message.

Envoys to Various Kingdoms

Envoys were sent to the rulers of al-Yamama, Bahrayn, 'Uman and the Governors of Damascus and Alexandria.

The ruler of Alexandria sent to the Apostle four slave girls, one of whom was Mary, the Coptic, mother of Ibrahim, the Apostle's infant son. An envoy was sent to Caesar, who was Heraclius, the titular Roman emperor, with his capital at Constantinople. The letter he carried for him contained the message sent to all kings. *Inter alia* it stated: 'God has sent me as a blessing to all men, so take a message from me. God have mercy on you. Do not hang back from me as the disciples hung back from Jesus, son of Mary.'

The Caesar took the letter, looked at it and then put it between his thighs and ribs. He ordered the chief of police to 'turn Syria upside down,' and bring him the nearest of the Apostle. When a Quraysh merchant was produced before Heraclius, the Caesar asked him about the Apostle and his claims. From fear he did not speak highly of the Prophet and said, 'Don't let him cause you anxiety; his importance is less than what you have heard.' After he had interrogated him the Caesar summed up and said:

> I asked you about his lineage and you alleged that it was pure and of your best and God chooses only a man of the noblest lineage as a prophet. Then I asked if any man of his family made similar claims and you said No. Then I asked if he had been robbed of dominion and made this claim to recover it, and you said No. Then I asked you about his followers and you said that they were the weak and poor and young slaves and women, and such have been the followers of the prophets in all ages. Then I asked if his followers left him and you said None. Thus is the sweetness of faith: it does not enter the heart and depart. Then I asked if he was treacherous and you said No; and truly if you have told me the truth about him he will conquer me on the ground that is beneath my feet,

and I wish that I were with him that I might wash his feet. Go about your business.[27]

Heraclius, it is said, ordered the Roman generals to assemble in a room and commanded that the doors be locked. Addressing them from a balcony he said:

. . . "O Romans, I have brought you together for a good purpose. This man has written me a letter summoning me to his religion. By God, he is truly the prophet whom we expect and find in our books, so come and let us follow him and believe in him that it may be well with us in this world and the next." As one man they uttered cries of disgust and ran to the doors to get out, but found them bolted. He ordered that they should be brought back to him, fearing for his life, and said: "I spoke these words that I might see the firmness of your religion in face of what has happened, and I am delighted with what I have seen of your behaviour." They fell down in obeisance and he ordered that the doors should be opened.[28]

Another version of the incident relates that Heraclius received the message from the Apostle at a time when he was on the move from Syria to Constantinople.

He gathered the Romans together and said: "I am laying before you some matters which I want to carry out. You know that this man is a prophet who has been sent; we find him in our book; we know him by his description, so come and let us follow him that it may be well with us in this world and the next." They said, "Are we to be under the hands of the Arabs when we are a people with a greater kingdom, a larger population, and a finer country?" He said, "Come and I will pay him the poll-tax every year and avert his onslaught and get rest from war by the money I pay him." They replied, "Are we to pay the low and insignificant Arabs a tax when we are more numerous, with greater sovereignty and a stronger country? By God, we will never do it." He said, "Then come and let me make peace with him on condition that I give him the land of Syria while he leaves me the land of Sha'm." Syria with them meant Palestine, Jordan, Damascus, Hims and what is below the Pass of the land of Syria, while what was beyond the Pass meant Sha'm. They said, "Are we to give him the land of Syria, when you know that it is the navel of Sha'm? By God, we will never do it." At this refusal he said, "You will see that you will be conquered when you protect yourself against him in your province."[29]

The two versions vary in detail but they agree that while the reactions of the Caesar to the Apostle's invitation were favourable, he failed to respond on account of the fear of his nobles who were opposed to the acceptance of Islam.

Chosro, the king of Persia, tore up the Apostle's letter. When the Prophet was informed of it he said, 'His kingdom will be torn to pieces.' Chosro wrote to his governor in Yaman to send 'two stout fellows to this man in the Hijaz and bring him to me.' The Governor of Yaman sent two messengers to the Apostle ordering him to go with them to Chosro. The two men came to the Apostle and told him that the 'king of kings' Chosro had written to his governor in Yaman ordering him to produce Muhammad before him. If he obeyed, they would write to the king on his behalf and keep him from him; but if he refused to come he knew what sort of man he was: he would destroy his people and lay waste his country. The Apostle ordered the messengers to come back to him the next morning. Meanwhile news was received that Shirawayh had killed his father Chosro. Thereupon he summoned the messengers and informed them of Chosro's death. They said: 'Do you know what you are saying? We can take revenge on you. What is easier? Shall we write this as from you and tell the king of it?' The Apostle said, 'Yes, tell him that from me and tell him that my religion and my sovereignty will reach limits which the kingdom of Chosro never attained. Say to him, "If you submit I will give you what you already hold and appoint you king over your people in the Yaman."' The governor of Yaman became a Muslim and one of his messengers who had been sent to arrest Muhammad said to him, 'I never spoke to a man for whom I felt more respect and awe.'

3

THE MORAL DIPLOMACY

GENTLENESS IN HUMAN RELATIONS

Muhammad's life was not one of renunciation. Every moment was crowded with activity. There were strains, trials, and many provocations. Yet the Prophet never lost hope or temper, even for a moment. The Qur'an defines a good Muslim as one who restrains his anger[1] or one who forgives when he is angry.[2] It is easy to forgive in a state of composure, but the merit lies in forgiving even when one is angry: 'Keep to forgiveness (O Muhammad) and enjoin kindness and turn away from the ignorant.'[3] The directive is to forgive injuries, insults and persecutions, to continue to declare the faith and act up to it in all situations; to pay no attention to ignorant people who raise doubts or difficulties, hurl taunts or reproaches, or intrigue and plot to defeat the truth; they are to be ignored and passed by, not to be engaged in disputes and fruitless controversies, or conciliated by compromises. One might think, on occasion, that revenge or retaliation, or a little tactful silence when evil stalks the land, or some compromise with ignorance, might be best for the cause. All such suggestions are to be rejected by a

Muslim, who should make no compromise with principles. But while he is firm and inflexible on the fundamentals of his faith, he is gentle and courteous and in fact forgiving while dealing with friends or foes. He avoids all vain discourse,[4] he invites and argues in ways most gracious,[5] his words are gentle,[6] his manner is graceful,[7] he is unfailing in courtesy, and he says what is best,[8] without hurting the susceptibilities of any person or party. The righteous man must not hide his light under a bushel, or compromise with evil, but while negotiating he must tackle the other party with the discretion and skill of a spiritual teacher. A Muslim is forbidden, therefore, from abusing even false gods, for those who worship them might turn around and revile God Himself.

Unlike the conventional diplomat who tends to assume a passive, noncommittal look, the Prophet always welcomed people with a smile and a salutation of peace. Gentle and soft-spoken, he took care to avoid expressions which might be construed, even by implication, as derogatory or contemptuous. He used simple language without an effort at creating effect. He spoke slowly and deliberately, pronouncing every word distinctly. There was a poise and dignity about his conversation but never any ambiguity. Muslims are expressly forbidden from using words of ambiguous import.[9] The Prophet permitted no mental reservations to himself and spoke with a clarity springing from the strength of his convictions. He always said what he considered just and correct. He refused to indulge in vain discourse; he was always brief and precise and never raised his voice to a high pitch. He reflected before he spoke, and when he spoke he had always a good word to say. He advised his followers to remain quiet if they did not have a good thing to say, implying thereby that one must always seek the good in human dealings. He warned his followers to beware of their tongues, for this weapon can be used both for good and for evil. Whoever exercises strict control over his tongue, he said, will attain to heavenly bliss. The Prophet avoided entering into long-winded arguments or indulging in lengthy speeches. He always practiced and commended brevity and moderation. Conversation should serve the purpose of clearly communicating one's thoughts. All ornamentation, exaggeration and dramatisation should be avoided. If an argument fails to carry conviction, the meeting should end without any bad blood. One should always be able to agree to disagree and tell those who differ:

> Unto us our works, and unto you your works,
> No argument between us and you.
> Allah will bring us together
> And unto Him is the journeying.[10]

Faith cannot be forced down a person's throat. A silly question need not be answered; it should be ignored. A good word, said the Prophet, is an act of charity, and a good man is he who develops a sweet reasonableness of speech which acts as a healing balm. A good word brings men together while a bad one rends them asunder. It provokes jealousy, hatred, disunity and discord. Muslims are exhorted to use good words in a good cause. 'A good word,' says the Qur'an, 'is like a goodly tree whose root is firmly fixed and its branches reach the heavens; it brings forth its fruit at all times, by the leave of its Lord.' The evil word, on the contrary, is like an evil tree which is torn up by the root from the surface of the earth and has no stability.[11] Muslims are therefore prohibited the use of figures of speech which cause irritation. 'Speak fair to the people,' is the motto of Islam.[12]

This, in brief, was the Prophet's approach. He was

as unruffled in Mecca when he was abused by Abu Jahl
as he was calm in Ta'if when he was bleeding in the
streets. To lose his temper was to lose the cause. Muhammad was as soft of speech as he was kind of heart. This was
the quality which helped him break the barriers of
hostility and gather around him a band of devoted followers whose loyalty to him was at once an asset and an
example. The Qur'an pays a great tribute to his temperament.[13]

The extremely gentle nature of Muhammad endeared
him to all; it was reckoned as one of the Mercies of God.
One of the Apostle's titles is 'A Mercy to all Creation.'
At no time was this gentleness, this mercy, this long-
suffering patience with human weakness more valuable
than after disasters like that of Uhud. Softness is always
to be preferred to severity, for strong words break no
bones but can wreck many a negotiation. The temptation
to retort and hit back is human, but those who succumb
to it make bad negotiators. The Prophet once received
a delegation of Jews who greeted him with the words
Assamu 'alaykum which means 'Death on you.' The expression in its sound and intonation much resembles
the Muslim form of salutation *Assalamu 'alaykum* (may
peace be on you) : eliminate the 'l' and the salutation of
peace changes into a curse. The Prophet's wife 'A'yesha
understood the import of the mischievous variation and
was quick to hit back by saying 'May death come to you
and may the curse of God be on you.' Muhammad lost
no time in admonishing his consort to keep her peace.
But she remonstrated in the belief that her husband had
not realised the mischief and pointed out the subtlety
involved in the phrase. The Prophet drew her attention
to his own reply with which he had acknowledged the
'greeting' of the Jews. It was a simple monosyllable meaning 'as on you.' Thus he conveyed the same meaning with

a gentle subtlety which 'A'yesha conveyed with a show of stern retaliation. The Prophet always practised and pleaded for perfect control of temper. An angry man is a social menace, but an angry diplomat is a national disaster.

'Ali, the first cousin and son-in-law of the Prophet, had the rare opportunity of living with the Apostle for some twenty-three years. Husayn, his son, once asked him about the character and temperament of the Prophet. This is what 'Ali told him:

> The Prophet was cheerful, gentle and kind by temperament. He was not stern, rigid or narrow-minded. He was not fussy and never shouted nor uttered a bad word. He did not pick holes in others nor did he encourage them to talk ill in his presence. When he did not like a certain remark, he made no loud protest but simply ignored it by silence. If somebody made an inappropriate request in the hope that he would grant it, he never disappointed him with an abrupt No. He just kept quiet and did not commit himself one way or the other. Those who knew him always understood the import of his silence. He had completely eliminated three things from his character: argumentation, unnecessary talking, and meddling in matters which did not concern him. While talking of others he always kept three considerations in mind—he never talked ill, he never picked holes and he never talked scandal. He only talked on subjects which could lead to some useful results. When the Prophet talked, his companions kept quiet and listened with rapt attention. They spoke only after he had finished. Only one person spoke at a time, and if someone else wanted to say something he waited for his own turn. If the people laughed at a certain remark the Prophet joined them with a smile but he never roared with laughter. If the people showed surprise at a certain thing, the Prophet joined them in expressing the same feelings. If some outsider stepped in and started speaking

crudely, the Prophet always tolerated him. He disliked listening to his own praise, but if someone offered thanks for a favour, he always acknowledged it. He never interrupted a person and always waited for him to finish. He was extremely pleasant and charming, strictly truthful, very generous and very gentle. If someone saw him suddenly for the first time he was overawed but as he came to know him he started loving him.

Another companion, Hind bin Abi Hala, who was literally brought up by the Prophet, has the following to say about the temperament of his master:

> He was gentle and good-tempered. He was never severe or stern nor did he ever consider it appropriate to offend anyone. He expressed gratitude at the most trivial things done for him. He never called anybody or anything bad— even when he did not like a meal, he did not criticise it but ate it with apparent relish. If somebody opposed the cause of truth he opposed him with all the might at his command but he never retaliated in matters concerning his own person—in such matters he could never be provoked; he never lost his temper nor did he ever seek revenge.

All contemporary sources are unanimous in their estimate of the Prophet. What emerges from their account is the radiant picture of a thorough gentleman— smiling, soft-spoken, sedate and sympathetic; dignified, considerate and calm; modest, humble and truthful; kind, hospitable and generous; fair, just and tolerant; simple and straightforward; courageous and contented. Muhammad always welcomed people with a smile and a warm handshake. He was always the first to greet, and was never the first to withdraw his hand but waited till the visitor released it. His capacity for suffering fools was surprising. He never betrayed his disapproval of their behaviour and suffered it with good cheer. There is the classic example of his marriage feast on the occasion of his wedding with Zaynab. The guests sat chatting long into the night after dinner. But he did not utter a word or make a movement which might have suggested that they were unwanted.

He never expressed his personal dislikes even when he felt them strongly. He never criticised a man for his personal failings and always made it a point to make him feel at home in his presence. He never pointed out a person even if he mentioned his failings in his congregational addresses. He always used the third person and never pointed his finger at anyone.

Once a notorious character sought an interview with him. The Prophet acknowledged he was a bad man but nevertheless allowed him an interview. During conversation with him, he was found to be extremely gentle and courteous to the visitor. His wife, to whom the Prophet had made the earlier remarks, was a bit surprised. She asked him why he had been so kind to a person who he knew was incorrigible in his evil ways. He replied, 'The worst man in the eyes of God is he whom people feel compelled to give up for his bad tongue!'

The Qur'an commands a Muslim: 'Be most modest in thy bearing and subdue thy voice. Lo! the harshest of all voices is the voice of the ass!'[14] The 'golden mean' is the kernel of the philosophy of Islam. In all things be moderate. Do not be talkative and do not be tongue-tied. Do not be loud and do not be timid. Do not be overconfident, and do not be cowed down. If you have patience, it is to give you constancy; if you have humility, it is to save you from unseemly swagger, not to curb your spirit and your reasoned determination.

The Bedouins were notoriously abrupt and crude in their manner. 'The Arabs of the desert,' says the Qur'an,

'are more hard in disbelief and hypocrisy, and most likely
to be ignorant.'[15] The Prophet owed some money to one
of them and when he came to ask for it, he behaved in a
manner which perhaps came naturally to him but shocked
the circle of the Prophet's companions. They were furious
at his impertinence, but the Prophet intervened with the
remark that their sympathies should be with the Bedouin
and not with him who owed money to him!

During the period when the Quraysh rebuked the
Prophet, threatened him with death, strewed thorns in
his way, poured filth on his body and put a noose round
his neck and, wielding all the weapons of injury and
insult, dubbed him a poet, a soothsayer, a man possessed
by a devil, a magician, they nevertheless failed to provoke him to anger or retaliation. The Prophet did not
even turn to look at Abu Jahl when he constantly followed him making it impossible for him to speak to a
gathering since he was always insulted and interrupted
by his unrepentant foe.

A Muslim must speak mildly under all circumstances:
in argument with an adversary, in talking to a friend, or
in conference with an opponent. Nowhere is he to show
impatience and use strong language, for in so doing he
will be ill serving his own cause. The Qur'an exhorts all
Prophets to be mild, even while talking to the most arrogant of men. Nobody could have been more inordinate
in his vanity and incorrigible in his arrogance than
Pharaoh who had indeed transgressed all bounds. Moses
and Aaron are charged with a mission to approach him
with these instructions:

> Go both of you, unto Pharaoh.
> Lo! he hath transgressed (the bounds)
> And speak unto him a gentle word,
> That peradventure he may heed.[16]

The negotiations of Moses with Pharaoh offer an inspiring example in patiently conducting the most tortuous of talks with a party notorious for its intransigence. The Qur'an records briefly the conversation between Moses and Pharaoh but there is a wealth of suggestion in this brief account. When Moses delivered his message the first question Pharaoh asked him was: 'Who, then, is the Lord of you twain?'[17] The implication of this question being that the God represented by Moses was not the Lord of Pharaoh who claimed the status of a demi-god for himself, was Moses, then, an emissary of the sun-god who was represented on earth by Pharaoh or was he an envoy of one of the many other gods in which the Egyptians believed? The question was pregnant with dangerous implications, and a hastily conceived answer, in the heat of the moment, could have set at naught the whole mission of Moses. But, instead of allowing himself to be involved in labyrinthine argumentation, Moses gave a simple and clear reply which was at once a direct answer to the question and an indirect refutation of all the basic beliefs of the Pharaoh and his people. The answer not only made a claim but also offered an argument in support of it. Moses told the Pharaoh:

> Our Lord is
> He who gave unto everything its nature,
> Then guided it aright.[18]

The answer of Moses is straight and simple. It is not evasive, ambiguous or insinuating. He would not dispute about 'my lord,' or 'your lord,' the God of Israel, or the God of Egypt. He is the emissary of 'our Lord,' Who created all beings and all things and from Whom each created being derived its nature—Pharaoh was sub-

ject to the same condition. Would he, then, understand
and accept the truth? But the Pharaoh was intransigent
and insisted on his provocations. He wanted to trap Moses
and involve him in discussion and argument. 'If,' he
says, in effect, 'there is only one God, to Whom all things
are referred, this is a new religion and I am not going
to accept it. What is the religion of your ancestors? Were
they all wrong in worshipping the Egyptian gods? And
if they were all wrong are they now in misery?' If Moses
could be provoked into a denunciation of Pharaoh's
ancestors, this would deprive him of the sympathy of
the Egyptian crowd. Intent upon involving and disgrac-
ing Moses before his people, Pharaoh came out with
another ingenious question. Pharaoh asked him:

> What then
> Is the state
> Of the generations of old?[19]

The question offered unlimited scope for argument and
discussion. If Moses had succumbed to the temptation
of answering it, he would have been caught in a trap.
But he remembered his instructions to speak mildly.
He replied:

> The knowledge thereof
> Is with my Lord,
> In a Record, my Lord
> Neither erreth, nor forgetteth.[20]

He spoke mildly but did not in any way whittle down
the truth. He finished the whole controversy in a sentence by refusing to enter a field which had no connec-
tion with his own brief. He was dealing with a subject

which was present in all its reality, and thus he could not be induced to ignore the facts of the situation in favour of a doubtful peep into the past. The Lord never errs nor forgets, and He would look to the actions of previous generations who would be dealt with according to this universal law. Why should he, then, get involved in a speculative discussion of a subject of which he had no knowledge and over which he exercised no control? And why should he not confine himself to dealing with a problem at hand instead of dabbling with a hypothetical question?

This is a leading principle of conduct which marks the approach of all prophets who pursue their mission without lending themselves to distracting discussions and controversies. The Qur'an offers a clear code of conduct for conveying one's message and conducting negotiations. The qualities it demands first of a negotiator are understanding and sympathy, mildness and moderation, love and understanding as opposed to force and compulsion, arrogance and conceit, intimidation and coercion. It inculcates persuasion as against the display of strength and severity. The other qualities it demands are patience and perseverance. One must proceed slowly and cautiously, one must show tolerance and possess a readiness to understand the point of view of one's opponent; one must aim at winning over his heart; and if one fails to carry conviction after all one's effort, one must remember that there is no coercion in Islam, and one's duty is to convey the message and not necessarily convert one's opponent to one's point of view.

> Thine is only to convey (the message) .[21]
> Remind them for thou art a remembrancer,
> Thou art not at all a warder over them.[22]

TRUST IN TRUTH

Diplomacy for the Prophet was but a means to an end, and he attached as much importance to the means as to the end itself. If the end was holy and worthy of noble sacrifice, it could not be achieved by employing unholy and ignoble means. He therefore gave a moral basis to diplomacy, and the art which was distrusted because of its inglorious record came to assume a mission and a meaning unfamiliar to its earlier adepts.

In wielding diplomacy, the Prophet did not deviate from the principles which guide the life of every believer. No principled man can do justice to the ends of peace if he pursues his mission in order merely to win acclaim or to escape censure. The fear and favour of men can be no guide to truth; and success alone is not the yardstick by which the efforts of an emissary should be measured. The Prophet in devoting himself wholeheartedly to his work could completely ignore these considerations, for it was not the favour of men that he sought, nor did he wish to escape their wrath—he only set out to serve the ends of peace, justice and truth regardless of the consequences. The faith that truth shall win and falsehood vanish inspired all his actions as it inspired the lives of those around him. Never did he commend an action or a thought without making it a part of his own life—he did what he said, and he always said what was best. Cultured, modest and dignified, the Prophet could conduct the most complicated of negotiations with calmness and a quiet demeanour with the highest degree of honesty and truth.

There is universal agreement about the moral stature of the Prophet. The details of his life are well known: his words as well as his deeds. He lived and worked among

Arabs who were steeped in ignorance and superstition—a people who lived in a world of their own, plundering, fighting, quarrelling—without any scruples. It was among these people that Muhammad lived and worked; through their crooked ways he walked straight and upright and won from them the title of *al-Amin*, the Man of Faith. This was long before he became a prophet. He laboured honestly, traded with integrity and mixed with every class of people, and even as a young man he came to have a reputation for the highest integrity. People gladly sought his help as a mediator in their complicated disputes and looked upon him as an amiable peacemaker. The extremely gentle nature of Muhammad endeared him to all. It was a godly quality, which then, as always, bound the souls of countless men to him. In no other profession is this gentleness, this mercy, this tolerance more essential and valuable than in the tedious and tortuous process of negotiations where the slightest show of temper, intolerance, severity or harshness might undo and destroy the results of all previous labour. The Prophet possessed these qualities and it was because of them that he was able to gather around him the most devoted followers that ever gathered around a leader. The Qur'an pays him the rare tribute:

> It is part of the Mercy
> Of God that thou dost deal
> Gently with them.[23]

Of all the qualities of a believer enumerated in the Qur'an, pride of place must be given to the quality of truth—truth in word and deed. A man devoted to truth is an honest man, a man of faith who is true to his word, a brave man with the courage of his convictions, removed from hypocrisy and intrigues, a man incapable of double dealings and impatient of flattery and intrigue. He inspires confidence in everyone with whom he deals. Cunning, trickery and guile have no place in the diplomacy of Islam. The Qur'an is explicit in its condemnation of all fraud, wherever it may exist—in little things of daily life or in the more subtle forms of political life. Diplomacy in Islam is a clean and fair game, an inalienable part of the greater game that is life. Indeed a Muslim looks at life as a trust from God—a trust which was offered to the heavens and the earth and the mountains but which they declined to accept.[24] Man accepted it and in so doing he undertook heavy responsibilities— it is he who has imposed this obligation on himself and if he fails now to discharge it, he will be guilty of a breach of faith.

> Those who faithfully observe
> Their trusts and other covenants.[25]

> And if one of you deposit a thing
> On trust with another,
> Let the trustee (faithfully discharge his trust).[26]

And the keeping of trust is not limited to money or property, as is generally understood; it embraces the whole field of our dealings—financial, legal, political and moral. If somebody confides a secret in you, it becomes a solemn trust which must not be betrayed; if somebody has consulted you in a certain affair, the matter must be kept to yourself. A person who betrays a trust, said the Prophet, is devoid of all faith, and a man who fails to keep his word is bereft of all moral values. A person who is capable of once betraying a trust loses his title to confidence for he can do it again.

So great is the stress on honesty and good faith that

it is impossible to imagine a good man without these qualities. In diplomacy they assume an added importance. 'Fulfil every engagement,' exhorts the Qur'an, 'for every engagement will be inquired into.'[27] Believers are described as 'those who fulfill the Covenant of God and fail not in their plighted word.'[28] They are commanded to 'fulfil all obligations.'[29] The command is comprehensive. The Arabic word for obligations, 'uqud, implies so much that a whole chapter could be written on it.

First, there are the divine obligations that arise from our spiritual nature and our relation to God. He created us and implanted in us the faculty of knowledge and foresight. . . . He made Nature responsive to our needs and His Signs in Nature are so many lessons to us for our own inner life; He further sent Messengers and Teachers, for the guidance of our conduct in individual, social and public life. All these gifts create corresponding obligations which we must fulfil. But in our own human and material life we undertake mutual obligations, express and implied. We make a promise; we enter into a commercial or social contract; we enter into a contract of marriage; we must faithfully fulfil all obligations in all these relationships. Our group or our State enters into a treaty: every individual in that group or State is bound to see that, as far as lies in his power, such obligations are faithfully discharged. There are tacit obligations: living in civil society, we must respect its tacit conventions unless they are morally wrong, and in that case we must get out of such a society. There are tacit obligations in the characters of host and guest, wayfarer or companions, employer or employed, etc., etc., which every man of Faith must discharge conscientiously. The man who deserts those who need him and goes to pray in a desert is a coward who disregards his obligations. All these obligations are inter-connected. Truth and fidelity are parts of religion in all relations of life.[30]

When a Muslim makes a commitment with an individual or a nation, his undertaking assumes the status of a covenant of God. In Islam the commitment of an individual has been made obligatory on the whole *ummah*. If he fails to abide by his word, he becomes guilty of a breach of trust. He is, therefore, commanded:

> Fulfil the Covenant of Allah when ye have covenanted, and break not your oaths after the asseveration of them, and after ye have made Allah surety over you. Lo! Allah knoweth what ye do.[31]

This is a universal rule covering all spheres of a man's life. In the individual sphere, we often see a man being punctilious in carrying out his personal commitments, but the same man, who feels so strongly about the moral value of a promise, does not feel any pangs of conscience in breaking his word on the level of a community, a nation or a state. On the contrary, such an act is acclaimed as a proof of political and national sagacity, particularly when it is directed against a hostile community. The real test lies, therefore, in the difficult and delicate task of carrying out commitments between communities. We have before us the example of the civilised world today. No greater affront to the self-respect of man could be offered in a civilised society than to call him unreliable and untrustworthy. An individual Englishman, Frenchman or German will display, for example, a remarkable respect for his commitments in his own daily dealings, but the same individual when he assumes a representative character often displays a surprising disregard for the moral values so conspicuous in his individual life. It is a paradox that an individual who does not tolerate a breach of faith with an individual in his private life feels no reluctance in gladly doing so where millions of men are concerned. He has one standard of morality for himself and another for his nation. Let us cite an example. The British character was coming to one of the high points in its history when, in the beginning of the eighteenth century, we on the Indian subcontinent came into contact with it. But while they set for themselves a high moral code in England, the code followed by them in India during the subsequent centuries was completely different. Every treaty which the British entered into with a powerful party was faithfully observed; every treaty which was signed with a weak party was, however, observed more in the breach. Treaties with Ammi Chand, Mir Ja'far, Mir Qasim, Shah-i-'Alam, Raja Chet Singh, Nawab Faydullah, Sa'adat 'Ali Khan, Nizam 'Ali Khan, Berar, Jaipur and the Mirs of Sind carried no value, and could be flouted at will because the other party was weak; but similar treaties with Haydar 'Ali, Holkar and Ranjit Singh assumed a moral value because the parties were strong. Commitments were honoured, therefore, not because they were commitments and had to be honoured, but because it became necessary to do so in the national interest. These were the considerations governing the conduct of one of the most civilised nations of the world.

This conduct in modern times finds a parallel in the Arabs before Islam. While on an individual level they were extremely scrupulous in observing their promises, they placed no value on them when it came to a communal or a tribal plane. Strength and power was honoured more than the moral value of a treaty. But Islam does not approve of this standard. One cannot have one set of values for oneself and another for those who do not belong to one's group. Islam lays down definite rules for human conduct in all its spheres. The party concerned may be an individual or a community, the matter may be personal or political, the person may be a relative or a stranger, a friend or a foe; he may be in or outside the fold of race or community; the time may be of peace or war—under no circumstances and under no pretext is a breach of trust permissible. Such an act must be condemned and severely punished irrespective of the circumstances. This is the reason why in characterising a believer, the quality of keeping faith is persistently stressed and a hypocrite is always marked out by his failure to keep his word. The sanctity of promises between two communities or nations receives an added stress in the Qur'an. You cannot lightheartedly enter into a commitment with a nation and then repudiate it because it has become weak, nor can you break your word with impunity. You cannot seek an alliance with a strong group which you think will be more useful for you if this course violates your treaty with another group which has since become weak and therefore in your opinion useless. It is imperative for a Muslim to honour his undertakings regardless of their effect on his immediate interests. In pursuing this course he should be prepared to brave dangers and suffer hardships, if that becomes necessary, but under no circumstances is he to go back on his word. There is a beautiful parable in the Qur'an which warns against such a course—the parable of a woman breaking into untwisted strands the yarn which she has spun after it has become strong. This is the example of a man or a group which enters into a treaty, gives all assurances, and does everything possible to ensure the strength of the bond. How can such a man or a group break and destroy all that he or it has achieved after laborious efforts at weaving and strengthening the threads of mutual bonds? How can such a man hope to inspire confidence after he has once broken his word? It costs a woman much labour and skill to spin good strong yarn. She would be foolish indeed to untwist its constituent strands and break them into flimsy pieces.

A Muslim is thus forbidden from using diplomacy in merely making his own party strong by violating alliances cemented by covenants when a stronger party offers him its alliance. Islam sets nobler standards for individuals and nations. A covenant must be looked upon as a solemn trust, not to be entered into except with the sincerest intention of carrying it out; and it is binding even if stronger nations are ranged against it:

> And be not like unto her who unravelleth the thread, after she hath made it strong, to thin filaments, making your oaths a deceit between you because of a nation being more numerous than (another) nation. Allah only trieth you thereby, and He verily will explain to you on the day of Resurrection that wherein ye differed.[32]

In our discussion of the Treaty of Hudaybiya we watched the threatening situation created by the dramatic appeal of Abu Jandal for protection; we also saw that the Prophet did not allow his judgment to be swayed by his sympathies. He surrendered a Muslim to the persecution of the Quraysh because that alone was consistent with the promise he had given them. An undertaking was honoured even though it appeared a callous step taken in disregard of Muslim interests. The intercession of statesmen like Abu Bakr and 'Umar was rejected because word had been given and word had to be kept. The sceptic might argue that there was no alternative because the Muslims in Hudaybiya had been caught unprepared by the threatening hordes of the Quraysh. Moreover, if the Prophet's insistence on a faithful execution of the treaty was governed at Hudaybiya by considerations of his own weakness and not by any inherent moral dictates of principle, the attitude should have changed with the accession of strength to Islam in the years that followed the treaty. With the growing strength of Muslims and the corresponding decline of the Quraysh in the years following the Treaty of Hudaybiya, it should not have been difficult for the Prophet to denounce the document, which was then considered by leading Muslims to be humiliating and disadvantageous to the interests of Islam. The period of their strength indeed offered a challenge to the character of Islam's early adherents. Their greatness lay in the fact that they honoured a treaty in the hour of their strength although they signed it in the hour of their weakness. Even though some contracting tribes had violated the treaty, the Muslims who were by now masters of Mecca were not allowed to retaliate without a long warning of four months. The Muslims scrupulously observed their part, but the pagans violated theirs time and again. After some years' experience it became imperative to denounce the treaty. But even then, it was done in due form, with four months' notice, and a chance to those who faithfully observed their pledges, to continue their alliance.

> Freedom from obligation (is proclaimed) from Allah and His Messenger towards those of the idolaters whom ye made a treaty: Travel freely in the land four months, and know that ye cannot escape Allah and that Allah will confound the disbelievers (in His guidance).[33]

The Muslim ruler cannot denounce a treaty unless he first informs the other party, and he cannot act in any way contrary to the treaty until reasonable time has passed, in which it is expected that the information has reached the central government of the other party.[34]

After the conquest of Mecca there was a general agreement between the Apostle and the polytheists that none should be kept back from the Ka'ba and that none need fear during the sacred month of pilgrimage. There were also particular agreements with the Arab tribes for specified terms. In A.H. 9 the Apostle sent Abu Bakr to lead the Muslims to Hajj while the polytheists were at their pilgrimage stations. After Abu Bakr had left, the mandate came down to the Prophet about the breaking of the agreement with the polytheists. He selected 'Ali to proclaim to the people on the day of sacrifice when they assembled at Mina. The proclamation, *inter alia*, made the following points:

No polytheists shall make pilgrimage after the year A.H. 9 and no naked person shall circumambulate the Ka'ba. He who has an agreement with the Apostle has it for his appointed time only. A period of four months from the date of the proclamation was given to the men to return to their place of safety or their country; afterwards there was to be no treaty or compact except for one with whom the Apostle had an agreement for a period, and he could have it for that period. After that year no polytheist went on pilgrimage or circumambulated the Ka'ba naked. This was the mandate in regard to the polytheists who had a general agreement, and also to those who had a respite for the specified period. Then the Apostle gave orders to fight the polytheists who had broken the special agreement as well as those who had a general agreement after the four months which had been given them as a fixed time.

With this sanction to denounce the treaty, emphasis is laid on the fact that the permission does not cover those who had given no occasion to deserve this repudiation and that they should, therefore, continue to receive the treatment due to them under the covenant.

Excepting those of the idolaters with whom ye (Muslims) have a treaty, and who have since abated nothing of your right nor have supported anyone against you. (As for those) fulfil their treaty to them till their term. Lo! Allah loveth those who keep their duty (unto Him).[35]

The duty of fulfilling all obligations of every kind is a cardinal feature of Muslim ethics. The problem of those who abuse this principle by failing in their duty but expecting the Muslims, nevertheless, to do their part is to be solved not by general denunciation of treaties but by a close and careful consideration of each case in which full care should be taken that the act of denunciation does not apply to those who have fairly played their part. In fact, steadfast adherence to a covenant under such conditions is hailed as an act of righteousness.

How can there be a treaty with Allah and with His Messenger for the idolaters save those whom Ye made a treaty at the Inviolable Place of Worship? So long as they are true to you, be true to them. Lo! Allah loveth those who keep their duty.[36]

This is the code which governed the conduct of the Prophet, both as a negotiator and as a man who was charged with the responsibility to ensure that covenants of every kind, entered into with God or His creatures, were to be honoured in all sincerity regardless of circumstances, which may at times appear to warrant abrogation in self-interest.

Muhammad emphasised moral integrity at a time when world morality was at a low ebb. He counted on moral influence as the most essential qualification of an envoy, who was not to permit himself to depart from honesty even though the dishonesty of others seemed apparently to justify such a course. Let us eschew evil, he preached, and not pay back evil in its own coin, however great the temptation; for two evils do not make a good. 'Repel evil with that which is best,' commends the Qur'an.[37]

The value of this lead given by the Prophet some fourteen hundred years ago will be realised when we notice that Western diplomacy, even after the rise of Islam, remained undecided on the question whether character, cunning or probity were the most effective instruments of diplomacy. Even some modern diplomats have sought to justify the diplomatic lie. Count Szilassy upholds it in certain circumstances. It is not until 1716 when Monsieur de Callieres published his treatise[38] that we notice an effort at pleading for credit and confidence in preference to deception. The history of European diplomacy in the eighteenth century gives the lie to the preaching of de Callieres, who wrote:

> The good negotiator will never base the success of his negotiations upon false promises or breaches of faith; it is an error to suppose, as public opinion supposes, that it is necessary for an efficient ambassador to be a past master in the art of deception; dishonesty is in fact little more than a proof of the smallness of mind of him who resorts to it, and shows that he is too meagrely equipped to gain his purpose by just and reasonable methods. Doubtless the art of lying has on occasions been successfully practised by diplomatists; but unlike the honesty which here, as elsewhere, is the policy, a lie always leaves in its wake a drop of poison. . . . Even the most dazzling diplomatic triumphs which have been gained by deception are based upon insecure foundations. They leave the defeated party with a sense of indignation, a desire to be revenged and a resentment which will always be a danger. Even were deceit not in itself repugnant to every right-minded per-

son, the negotiator should recollect that he is likely for the rest of his life to be constantly engaged in diplomatic business, and that it is essential for him to establish a reputation for straight and honest dealing so that thereafter man may be ready to trust his word.

It is only in the nineteenth century that we find a Western diplomat discovering through experience that duplicity does not pay in negotiations.

Lord Malmesbury had the following opinion to offer on diplomatic conduct:

> It is scarcely necessary to say that no occasion, no provocation, no anxiety to rebut an unjust accusation, no idea —however tempting—of promoting the object you have in you—can need, much less justify, a falsehood. Success obtained by one is a precarious and baseless success. Detection would ruin, not only your own reputation for ever, but deeply wound the honour of your Court. If, as so frequently happens, an indiscreet question, which seems to require a distinct answer, is put to you abruptly by an artful minister, parry it either by treating it as an indiscreet question, or get rid of it by a grave and serious look; but on no account contradict the assertion flatly if it be true, or admit it as true, if false and of dangerous tendency.

Here again we see no recognition of the moral virtue of truth which has been reduced to the level of a mere diplomatic device, to be used among others as the occasion demands. But Islam is not so lukewarm about the value of this quality. It does not look upon truth as a maid of convenience but as a master of men. Truth is a high moral virtue, a powerful weapon, which was wielded with great effect by the Prophet in the eternal war between the forces of good and evil.

The Qur'an compares truth to a goodly tree, firmly

established on its roots, stretching its branches high and wide, and bearing nothing but good fruit at all times.

> Seest thou not how Allah coineth a similitude of a goodly saying as a goodly tree, its root set firm, its branches reaching into heaven, giving its fruit at every season by permission of its Lord? Allah coineth similitudes for mankind in order that they may reflect. And the similitude of a bad saying is as a bad tree, uprooted from the earth, possessing no stability.[39]

In the life of Muhammad we see these lofty principles translated faithfully into action. The later development of diplomacy in Muslim countries has little relationship with the source. The statecraft of Nizam al-Mulk, for example, is not far removed from that of Machiavelli, and the performance of later diplomats in Islam brings little credit to the faith in the name of which they function. Barring a few honourable exceptions, the diplomatic methods and standards set up by the Umayyad and subsequent Caliphs, the Sultans and the Amirs are not different from the conduct of contemporary rulers in the Western world. It is particularly rewarding, therefore, to reflect upon the example of Muhammad in whose life we find an inspiring example.

FAITHFUL COMMUNICATION

Intellectual inaccuracy often springs from relying on the oral word; it also springs from an unwillingness to face unpleasant facts and an inability to experience and act on several different levels of reality at the same time. Distinguished diplomats have been known to be guilty of such inaccuracies. We have only to look to Bjorkoe, Buchlau, Thoiry, Stressa and Munich to realise how lofty mansions of peace can collapse simply because of a verbal equivocation which has cloaked differences of substance. Memory is an elusive friend and should never be trusted too long. Every conversation, every undertaking, every word given to another man should be reduced to writing at the first opportunity. The habit of writing down all commitments, even though inconvenient for a while, pays rich dividends. The unlettered Prophet, himself unable to write, insisted that all but trivial transactions should be reduced to writing. We have earlier seen the stress laid by Islam on a faithful discharge of contractual obligations. It is in the fitness of things, therefore, to insist on writing down all obligations, for probity in worldly matters is not a matter of mere convenience—it is a matter of conscience and religious duty. Even our everyday transactions are carried out in the presence of God, and if we attempt to deceive His creatures we will certainly not succeed in deceiving Him, for He knows all that is going on in the innermost recesses of our minds. An elaborate law is therefore laid down for writing down all obligations except those which involve a transaction completed on the spot.

O ye who believe! when you contract a debt for a fixed term, record it in writing. Let a scribe record it in writing between you in (terms of) equity. No scribe should refuse to write as Allah had taught him, so let him write, and let him who incurreth the debt dictate, and let him observe his duty to Allah his Lord, and diminish naught thereof. But if he who oweth the debt is of low understanding, or weak, or unable himself to dictate, then let the guardian of his interest dictate in (terms) of equity. And call to witness, from among your men, two witnesses. And if two men be not (at hand) then a man and two women, of such as ye approve as witnesses, so that if the one erreth (through forgetfulness) the other will remind her. And the witnesses must not refuse when they are summoned. Be not averse to writing down (the contract) whether it be small or great, with (record of) the terms thereof. That is more equitable in the sight of Allah and more sure for testimony, and the best way of avoiding doubt between you; save only in the case when it is actual merchandise which ye transfer among yourselves from hand to hand. In that case it is no sin for you if ye write it not. And have witnesses when ye sell one to another, and let no harm be done to scribe or witness. If ye do (harm to them) lo! it is sin in you. Observe your duty to Allah. Allah is teaching you. And Allah is knower of all things.[40]

These instructions safeguard against the danger of intellectual inaccuracy. But how about moral inaccuracy? This takes many forms. To analyse a situation by writing a report in a Delphic style—'Heads I win, tails you lose' type of a dispatch which commits nobody—is to evade responsibility. But this is a negative failing which springs from a lack of confidence in one's own judgment. A positive example of moral imprecision in a diplomat assumes the shape of an alarming tendency to water down his instructions when they are not entirely to his own liking and when he thinks that a faithful communication of those views would cause irritation to the country to which he is accredited. In other words, it is the case of a messenger trying to tamper with a message which he is charged to deliver.

Both the cases are covered by a lack of confidence in one's own moral integrity. Both spring from a weakness of character which betrays love of opportunism in preference to love of truth. An expedient approach—

departing from the spirit of one's instructions—is foreign to the fundamentals of the Islamic conception of diplomacy. The Prophet received a message—the most unpalatable message that an envoy could be asked to deliver to a nation. Once he had accepted the trust, it was not for him to seek evasion and escape the responsibility which ensued. When he received instructions to 'expound openly what thou art commanded,'[41] he ascended the Mount of Safa and delivered the message. He faced failure but in doing so he scored a victory. Not a soul among those assembled beneath the mountain challenged his integrity—all bore witness to his love of truth even though none of them accepted the truth which he expounded. In the wake of his failure came the directive to 'admonish thy nearest kinsmen.'[42] The Prophet proceeded to invite them to a meal at his house; his hospitality was returned by humiliating jeers when he delivered the message. The only person who agreed with him was his young cousin 'Ali—a lad of thirteen. But did he change his message because nobody of any consequence agreed with him? Hostility hardened, pressure increased, and a time arrived when Muhammad faced the prospect of losing his only support—the aged uncle who had brought up the orphan with such loving care. Abu Talib yielded to the mounting pressure of public opinion and agreed to stop his ward from indulging in activities which hurt the susceptibilities of the pagan Quraysh. The nephew was given a hint to drop his mission. 'Life of thine uncle!' entreated Abu Talib, 'do not place on me a burden greater than I can bear.' The appeal was sincere and deeply emotional. It did not fail to move Muhammad. With tears in his eyes he communicated his decision to his faltering uncle. 'By God,' he declared, 'if these people place the sun in one hand of mine and the moon in the other, they will not see me shirk from my duty. Either God will complete this Mission or I shall fall a martyr to the cause.'

The temptation of a diplomat to water down his instructions is persistent and hard to resist when personal popularity is at stake. He hesitates to take a step or convey a message which may prove distasteful to the country to which he is accredited. Nothing can be more dangerous than this tendency. A diplomat who treats his instructions with scant regard and carries them out with mental reservations lacks moral calibre.

We have seen the Prophet as a faithful envoy, but we should also study his reactions when he is called upon to convey a message involving a censure of his own conduct—the most trying test of moral precision. There are five occasions in the life of the Prophet when he was reprimanded for some minor decisions of a personal nature. But even minor decisions can have far-reaching repercussions when they are taken by a prophet. It becomes necessary, therefore, to correct and point out such minor lapses. The Qur'an was quick in seizing upon such opportunities and never failed to dwell on them.

An incident of this nature occurred while Muhammad was still in Mecca. He was earnestly engaged in preaching to the Quraysh. According to his own assessment of the situation, by far the best approach was for him to make an attempt at converting the Quraysh nobles to his point of view. Once this was achieved and the leaders were brought around, the rest would follow. However, the vain and proud leaders of the Quraysh shunned his company for he was always surrounded by the common men, tailors, butchers and shopkeepers, who shared his company—an innovation impossible for the traditional aristocracy of the Quraysh to suffer. Muhammad mustered all his powers of eloquence, nimbleness and incisiveness in pressing home his argument, and presented his case effectively. The Quraysh listened to him with rapt attention—in itself a reassuring proof of his success, for never before had he received a patient hearing from these impatient leaders. Now he could read sympathy and understanding writ large on the faces of his audience. Here was an occasion which could be used with effect. There came a time during the course of his address when Muhammad thought that the battle had been nearly won; but precisely at that moment in came a poor blind Muslim, oblivious of the effect which his intrusion would create. He had come in all sincerity to consult his leader, but little did he realise that he was doing so at an inopportune moment. The Prophet, who was determined to devote his undivided attention to the Quraysh, decided to ignore the interruption. Brushing aside the question raised by the poor Muslim, the Prophet continued to address the Quraysh, who were already feeling uncomfortable because of the meddlesome man who had dared to violate the sanctity of their aristocratic gathering by thrusting his presence on them. The Prophet was immediately taken to task by the Qur'an for showing preference to nobles and ignoring a sincere humble Muslim whose honest faith was more valuable than the hypocrisy of the nobility. There could be no distinction between the rich and the poor in Islam, and the Prophet in his zeal to further the cause was violating his instructions. This is how the Qur'an has summed up the episode:

He frowned and turned away
Because the blind man came unto him.
What could inform thee but he might grow (in grace)
Or take heed and so the reminder might avail him?
As for him who thinketh himself independent,
Unto him thou payest regard.

Yet it is not thy concern if he grow not (in grace)
But as for him who cometh unto thee with earnest purpose
And hath fear,
From him thou art distracted.
Nay, but verily it is an Admonishment,
So let whosoever will pay heed to it.[43]

The instructions clearly reproved Muhammad for the natural enthusiasm that had led him to an inappropriate step in his mission.

Another incident occurred in the early years of the Prophet's life in Medina. The occasion was the miraculous victory of a handful of Muslims over the overwhelming forces of the Quraysh in the battle of Badr. Poor and persecuted for thirteen years, Muslims came to know for the first time an experience which goes with victory. They had vanquished those who had driven them out from Mecca. As many as seventy of the Quraysh were now in captivity as their prisoners of war. Among them were 'Aqil, the brother of 'Ali, and 'Abbas, the Prophet's uncle, who was later to lend his name to the celebrated Abbasid dynasty. The temptation was great. The spectres of division, greed and personal aggrandizement were raising their ugly heads. The Muslim camp resounded with cries of revenge. A section insisted that the captives be burned alive. No less a person than 'Umar suggested that the prisoners of war should be put to the sword. But all these suggestions were firmly overruled by the Prophet, who decided to take ransom for the captives. Those who could not afford to secure their freedom in this way were released on agreeing to teach a few children in return for their liberty.

The ransom money was considerable—it was calculated to bring some forty thousand *dirhams* to a handful of poor Muslims. But a Muslim is not permitted to wage war except in self-defence or in defence of his faith. The greed for gain, therefore, in the shape of ransom from captives finds no place in his fighting. But there was no such rule at the time of Badr, and a decision had to be taken. The decision was later upheld and the Prophet was given complete discretion, but not before he was reproved for conferring freedom on his captives in return for ransom money.

> It is not for any Prophet to have captives until he hath made slaughter in the land. Ye desire the lure of this world and Allah desireth (for you) the Hereafter, and Allah is Mighty, Wise.
>
> Had it not been for an ordinance of Allah which had gone before, an awful doom had come upon you on account of what ye took.[44]

The revelation reproved Muhammad for an error of judgment which was later upheld and made a rule. But having received the reprimand he did not hesitate to publish and release this revelation, even though it censured his own action.

The third incident occurred in A.H. 9, the year of the Muslim expedition to Tabuk, the first challenge to Islam by an organised state. The challenge came at a time when famine stalked the land and oppressive heat was taking a heavy toll of life. The adherents of the Prophet, nevertheless, rose to unprecedented heights of loyalty and sacrifice when the call came from the leader. Each vied with the other in contributing to the cause. This was the occasion when 'Uthman offered two hundred camels besides a heap of silver and Abu Bakr came out with everything he had in his possession—including the buttons of his shirt. Thirty thousand Muslims marched out to meet the danger. Those who could not afford to equip themselves for the expedition remained remorsefully behind. Tears streamed down their eyes as they saw their brethren move out to meet the enemy. It is to these men, anxious to serve but unable to secure a chance, that the Qur'an refers in moving terms.[45]

While the Muslims rose to great heights of faith and devotion, the hypocrites among Muslims in Medina did their worst to sabotage the whole effort. Not only did they advance excuses to secure exemption from joining the expedition on false pretexts, they also organised a whispering campaign to demoralise Muslim volunteers by exaggerating the dangers of heat in the long weary journey which was to take them two hundred miles away from their homes. All their intrigues were foiled by the stunning response of the followers of the Prophet.

The hypocrites, adept in the arts of guile and intrigue, lost no time in presenting themselves individually to the Prophet in order to explain to him the circumstances which had led to their inability to join in. Everyone, it seemed, had a ready excuse which sounded convincing. The Prophet, true to his nature, abounding in mercy and goodwill, forgave all the hypocrites who had failed to join the expedition. The Prophet was actuated by motives of kindness as well as policy, because if anyone did not come with hearty goodwill, he would be a burden instead of a help to the army. The policy was justified, because in fact 30,000 men or more followed him. Nevertheless the Prophet received a mild rebuke for his policy of liberal exemptions:

> Allah forgive thee (O Muhammad)! Wherefore didst thou grant them leave ere those who told the truth were manifest to thee and thou didst know the liars?[46]

The Prophet did not attempt to justify his own stand or communicate the revelation with any comment indicating his disagreement with it. He faithfully conveyed the message, even though it appeared to censure his own conduct.

The life of Muhammad is a remarkable example of a well-integrated and harmonious whole which admitted of no false divisions and reservations. He was just and upright in all his dealings, and he exhorted others by his own example to emulate him. He conveyed the message most sincerely even though at times it reproached his own conduct; he acted on his instructions most faithfully even though he had to undergo endless suffering and sacrifice. He warned those who succumbed to the temptation of moral imprecision and perverted the Word of God knowingly after they had understood it. It is to such people who water down their instructions, or read into them what they want and project their own conjectures, or substitute their own word for their instructions, that the Qur'an refers as people trafficking with their conscience. Such people are losers even if they 'gain the whole world' for they lose their souls:

> Therefore woe be unto those who write the Scripture with their hands and they say, "This is from Allah," that they may purchase a small gain therewith. Woe unto them for that their hands have written, and woe unto them for that they earn thereby.[47]
>
> Lo! those who hide aught of the Scripture which Allah hath revealed, and purchase a small gain therewith, they eat into their bellies nothing else than fire.[48]

PATIENCE FOR A CAUSE

Patience does not consist in passive endurance of helplessness in the face of provocation; it is a calm endurance of pain or provocation but with a studied perseverance in the pursuit of an objective. It is the strength of the cause which lends strength to the capacity for patience. It is important that a diplomat be convinced, in the first instance, of the cause he is pleading, for without a deep faith in his own mission he cannot hope to carry conviction to others. He must then remain steadfast and hold his judgment, for if he starts anticipating he would be risking premature failure. A diplomat must continue with a singleness of purpose to pursue his mission. Distractions and distresses should not be permitted to divert him from his duty.

Waiting for the proper time is a characteristic of diplomacy. The phase of negotiations when a negotiator starts to lose patience with himself is the beginning of the end; the stage where he loses patience with others is most certainly the end itself. Nothing can be more disastrous in diplomacy than short temper. The world recalls with horror occasions when diplomats have lost their temper. Napoleon flung his hat on the carpet in the Marcoloni Palace at Dresden while negotiating with Metternich. Sir Charles Smith tore up a treaty with the Sultan of Morocco in the imperial presence. Count Tattenback lost his temper at the Algeciras Conference and exposed his country to grave humiliation. Such a show of impatience defeats the cause. It reveals the weakness of the cause which fails to inspire self-control in the men who seek to advance it.

No man who had a cause to espouse was ever surrounded with greater difficulties than the Prophet in Mecca, where he faced ordeals and suffered persecution for no less than thirteen years. The entire land offered nothing but naked hostility; nothing but dismal failure seemed to emerge from an environment of ignorance, cruelty and prejudice. What, then, could a man do under such circumstances? Should he give up the cause which he believed to be true or persevere in his efforts in the hope of success to come in its own proper time? The latter course is clearly ordained: 'So, wait patiently (O Muhammad) for the Lord's decree, for surely thou art in Our sight.'[49]

The man of God must strive his utmost; as for results, it is not for him to anticipate them. He must wait patiently in the sure knowledge that his cause is righteous, that he is constantly under the eyes of God. While he works without being able to secure spectacular results, he should not permit his faith to be weakened by success slipping for a time in the other direction. If he wavers or falters, success will evade him. Patience and perseverance alone will lead him slowly but surely to the cherished goal.

> So have patience (O Muhammad) : Allah's promise is the very truth, and let not those who have no certainty make thee impatient.[50]

The Prophet is cautioned against hasty action and is commanded to remain inflexible in his purpose regardless of the odds and difficulties which beset his path:

> Then have patience (O Muhammad) even as the stout of heart among the messengers (of God) had patience.[51]

Patience indeed is one of the cardinal virtues of a Muslim. But man is hasty by nature. The story of Saul in the Qur'an beautifully illustrates the point that those who cannot be patient are not capable of rising to any heights. When Saul set forth with his army to fight Goliath, he told his men that only those that did not drink from a stream which fell on the way would be allowed to accompany him in his expedition. The intention was to test their capacity for patience and endurance. Most of them failed, but those who persevered vanquished the much larger forces of Goliath.

Moses tends to lose his patience. He loses it with the man[52] who scuttles a boat, kills an innocent boy, and raises a falling wall in an inhospitable village. These acts, even though done by his spiritual leader, exasperate him because he fails to understand their motive. He was asked, therefore, to hold his patience or part company with his teacher. Again, he loses patience with his own brother (Aaron) who was entrusted with the leadership of Israel during his brief absence on the Mount of Sinai. In fact, he violently pulls his beard in asking for an explanation of his conduct which he brands as cowardly. A man of such violent disposition is commanded to be mild and patient with Pharaoh, the most arrogant of men that ever lived in history.

Negotiations are trying enough in any circumstances, but when dealing with an unreasonable party it is all the more essential to be patient. Even trivial and commonplace things sometimes assume perplexing proportions when it comes to negotiating a deal. The Bani Israel had every reason to be grateful to Moses who had led them out of slavery and servitude to the glory of freedom. But he needed all his patience and calm to get them to sacrifice a cow. They put him off on one pretext or another—what was the age of the cow, what was its colour, did it till the soil or water the fields?—questions put merely for the sake of evasion and not for any desire for information, a technique which is all too common in modern conferences. A simple request is received with carping criticism—objections are raised, explanations are sought, pretences are erected and questions are asked which would tax the patience of the calmest of men to the breaking point. But Moses is not exasperated into a show of temper in dealing with an ungrateful people. He meets all their points with patience till they offer the sacrifice, even though the will is still wanting. Patience in negotiations thus triumphs over a wavering people who are caught in the cobweb of their own cunning. Moses was constantly harassed with foolish, impertinent or disingenuous questions by his own people. Muslims are asked not to follow their example. 'Would ye question your Apostle as Moses was questioned of old?'[53]

MODESTY AND MODERATION

Vanity is a vice which springs from an exaggerated consciousness of one's qualities and importance and leads one to an ostentatious display in the belief that others either do not possess those qualities or have them in a measure which deserves neither recognition nor respect. Iblis was the first to make an empty boast of his attainments when he claimed superiority over Adam in that he had been created out of fire and man was made out of clay. Satan thus became the first, though not the last, votary of vanity. Vanity is of course a relative term. It is not the desire for achievement nor its consciousness in an individual which marks him out as a vain person. He becomes so only when a consciousness of his own attainments leads him to act or behave towards others in a manner which suggests that he considers them his inferiors. The difference between the two attitudes was brought out with precision by the Prophet when a very handsome man confided in him his own awareness of his attainments, which he was keenly jealous to guard. 'Does this attitude signify vanity?' he asked. 'Not at all,' replied the Prophet; 'vanity is a refusal to recognise reality, and to look down upon others as inferior.'

All vanity of colour and complexion, wealth and valour, riches and numbers, race and tribe is demolished by Islam. One cannot build on insubstantial foundations, and nothing is as unreal and empty as the claim of superiority dictated by vanity. It is through service alone that one can become superior, and those who serve are not vain.

The dangers of vanity in a diplomat can scarcely be exaggerated. The entire atmosphere of his life—the ceremonials, the court functions, the lavish receptions—all induce increasing vanity. Of the many diplomatic faults personal vanity is easily the most common. A diplomat who is honest, truthful, tactful, precise, patient and calm may yet fail to be an ideal diplomat if he is vain. Vanity in a negotiator tempts him to disregard the advice or opinions of those who may have had longer experience of a country, or of a problem, than he possesses himself. It renders him vulnerable to the flattery or the attacks of those with whom he is negotiating. It encourages him to take too personal a view of the nature and purposes of his functions and in extreme cases to prefer glittering but illusory triumph to some unostentatious but more prudent compromise. It leads him to boast of his victories and thereby to incur the hatred of those whom he may apparently have vanquished. It may prevent him, at some crucial moment, from confessing to his government that his predictions or his information were incorrect. It prompts him to incur or to provoke unnecessary friction over matters which are of no more than social importance. It may cause him to offend by ostentation, snobbery or vulgarity. It is at the root of all indiscretion and of most tactlessness. It lures its addict into such fatal diplomatic indulgences as irony, epigrams, insinuations and the barbed reply. It may induce that terrible and frequent illusion of the professional diplomat that his own post and person are the centre of the diplomatic universe. It may bring in its train those other vices of imprecision, excitability, impatience, emotionalism and even untruthfulness. Among the misfortunes into which vanity drives the frail spirit of man there is one which has a more specific bearing upon the art of negotiation. It is complacency. It leads first to a loss of adaptability, then to a decline in imagination. It is this rigidity of spirit which, as it settles upon the less gifted diplomat, deprives him of his adaptability. He fails to respond with needful elasticity to conditions of which he disapproves or to ideas with which he is not familiar.

Muhammad was born an orphan; he lost his mother as a child. He grew up under the loving care of his grandfather. With the latter's death, he came under the roof of his uncle where he spent his youth. With his marriage, at the age of twenty-five, he moved to the house of his wife who was a wealthy lady of Mecca. All that he inherited was a small house of his own which was snatched away from him by his cousin 'Aqil, the step-brother of 'Ali. He did not have a house of his own when he entered Mecca as a conqueror. In Medina he stayed at first in a small room in the house of Abu Ayyub Khalid bin Zayd Ansari; later he built himself a modest house adjacent to the mosque. It is in that house that he died and it is there that he lies buried in peace today. At the height of his glory when he could well afford a palace, he lived in a mud house thatched with branches and leaves of datepalm. If a person stood up in the room, he could easily touch the ceiling with his hand. Rain trickled down the roof which had to be protected by a blanket made out of camel hair. A mat, a leather pillow stuffed with palm fronds and a few skins hanging on the wall—this was all the furniture adorning the house of the ruler of Arabia. When a coloured curtain was hung in the house he ordered it to be removed; and 'A'yesha, who had taken the initiative, incurred the displeasure of the Prophet, who told her that he had not been entrusted with public money to clothe bricks and stones. The occasions when the family had to forgo a meal were not infrequent. He died clad in a coarse shirt and a blanket full of patches— this was the dress in which he received delegations in the unostentatious courtyard of his mosque.

The Prophet was an embodiment of modesty. He conducted himself with marked humility. He created a society which excluded all privilege. The only privilege lay in service and sacrifice. He made it a point to emphasise that he took no precedence over others. He never made himself conspicuous in any gathering. He sat with the common man and refused to arrogate to himself any rank of distinction. When he sat with others he made sure that his own knees were in line with them. When he went to visit someone he always avoided sitting in a conspicuous place. Once when the Prophet went to visit him in his house, 'Abdullah the son of 'Umar brought forth a leather cushion for him. But he sat down on the ground, and the cushion remained between him and his host. The Prophet issued strict instructions against the Persian custom of standing up with folded hands, a mark of respect for the rich. 'Whoever likes people standing thus in his presence,' he said 'should seek a place for himself in hell.' While he did not like others to show subservience to him, he himself stood up on occasions to greet and welcome those he loved. He was so inconspicuous sitting among his companions in the mosque that strangers coming from long distances to pay him homage had often to ask others who the Prophet was and where he was sitting. He greeted the rich and the poor alike. There was no discrimination between black, brown and white. Everybody who came to him was welcomed with a greeting and a smile. He went to the house of the poorest and exerted himself to entertain a person when he came to his own house. It often happened that the guest was fed and the Prophet and his family went without a meal. He was always the first to salute, and while walking in the street he greeted everybody, men, women and children, with a blessing for peace. He did not suffer from smugness or self-importance nor did he suffer from a sense of lofty superiority, for does not the Qur'an command:

> Turn not thy cheek in scorn towards folk, nor walk with hauteur in the land. Lo! Allah loveth not each braggart.[54]

Insolence, arrogance and undue elation at our powers or capacities lead to many evils. The man of God avoids these pitfalls for he knows that his gifts are from God. He is, therefore, always humble and modest in the whole outlook of his life. The Qur'an clearly lays down: 'And walk not in the earth exultant. Lo! thou cannot rend the earth, nor canst thou stretch to the height of the hills.'[55]

The Prophet disliked praise and flattery and never failed to nip the evil in the bud when somebody started indulging in it in his presence. Once he was talking about a person when one of the audience started praising that person in the superlative. 'You have cut the throat of your friend,' said the Prophet, repeating the sentence a number of times. Once on coming into the mosque he found a person engaged in prayers. He inquired about his name from a companion called Mihjan Thaqafi. While giving the information the companion accompanied it by profuse praise of the man. The Prophet was quick to point out that if the man were to listen to his own praise, he would be ruined. Once a poet Aswad bin Sari' came to the Prophet and asked for permission to recite a poem he had composed in praise of God and His Apostle. 'God likes praise,' said the Prophet, and Aswad started reciting his poem. Meanwhile somebody interrupted. When the man left, the poet resumed his recitation. The same person turned up after some time and the poet had to stop once again. This happened three or four times; and the poet who was upset by now asked in desperation the name of the man who had interrupted him so much to his annoyance. The Prophet replied that he was a man who disliked futile talk!

While the Prophet was averse to all forms of renunciation he was equally opposed to luxurious life and constantly pleaded for moderation. His own life was an example of simplicity and austerity. It was through sheer modesty and not because of poverty that he lived a humble life. He always wore simple clothes.

Widows were his particular concern and he often left his own work to do theirs. But when someone did the most trivial thing for him, he acknowledged it with an unfailing expression of gratitude. He sat and ate on an equal level with the poorest. He squatted like a humble slave and never made a movement which suggested anything like pride or vanity. 'I am a slave (of God),' he said, 'and I sit humbly like a slave. God has made me obedient and not proud and vain.' Once a person, overawed by the personality of the Prophet, started trembling in his presence. He reassured him with the words: 'I am not a king. I am the son of an ordinary woman of the Quraysh who used to eat dry meat.' He reprimanded a man who addressed him as 'Our Lord, the best among

us and son of the best among us.' 'Do not be led astray
by Satan,' he admonished; 'I am Muhammad, the son of
'Abdullah, the servant and Apostle of God. Do not add
a bit to the dignity that I have been given by God.'
Similarly, a person once addressed him as 'the best of
creation.' He replied that that applied to Abraham! We
have it on the authority of 'Abdullah bin Sakhir that
while he accompanied the embassy of Bani 'Amir, he
addressed the Prophet as 'My Lord.' The Prophet admonished him not to follow the ways of Satan! When
Muhammad entered Mecca at the head of the victorious
army of Islam, he hung his head in humility. At the
hour of his greatest glory he celebrated it by praising
God and asking His forgiveness. He rode a donkey while
marching to Khaybar as conqueror. He did not exult in
his triumph as he did not despair in defeat. All that was
good came from God as a blessing and all that was evil
came from one's self. He never lost an opportunity, therefore, to impress on his adherents that he was merely a
man like other men, with the difference that he conveyed
to them the message of God. He was never tired of pro-
claiming the words of the Qur'an:

> I have no power to benefit,
> Nor power to hurt,
> Save that which Allah
> Willeth. Had I knowledge of the Unseen,
> I should have abundance of wealth, and adversity could
> not touch me.
> I am but a warner and a bearer of good tidings unto
> folk who believe.[56]

'He appeared,' says Daumer, 'not as a son of Allah,
but only as His Prophet; he declared loudly that he was
a man like his fellow-men, and only had a mission from

God. Animated by this idea, he acted and united in himself great and noble qualities. Endowed with an inflexible will-power and an ardent spirit, tempered by compassion, charity and tenderness, he undertook the difficult mission and the stupendous struggles connected with it, and he did not rest until he had attained what he wanted: until Arabia professed his Faith. His behaviour became now the standard for his people also after his death. Inexorable against his enemies as long as they opposed him, yet he did not know the spirit of revenge; he was gentle towards the vanquished, indulgent and tolerant to all unbelievers.'[57]

Once he heard some girls sing a song during the marriage of a daughter of a companion. The song contained a line in praise of the Prophet. 'Leave this line,' said he, 'and sing the rest.' The sun happened to be eclipsed on the day of the death of Ibrahim, the Prophet's infant son whom he loved deeply. The people, always quick at believing and spreading a superstition, connected this incident with Ibrahim's death. It was God's condolence in his bereavement. The Prophet was prompt in removing the impression. He announced that an eclipse was a phenomenon of nature. It was foolish to attribute it to the birth or death of a human being.

Once the Prophet was performing his ablutions. The people around him collected the flowing water and rubbed it on their bodies. 'Why are you doing this?' inquired the Prophet. 'For the love of God and His Apostle!' He told them that they should seek it in truth and trust, honesty, honour and good-neighbourliness.

Such a man was Muhammad—sympathetic and considerate to the point of self-denial; charming and hospitable to a fault; always ready to help and always willing to see the other man's needs and point of view. Humble at the height of his glory and hopeful in the hour of defeat, he struggled till the end of his days with a singleness of purpose and left to posterity an example which will continue to inspire humanity with courage, hope and faith.

LOYALTY

Loyalty is an attitude of steadfast and consistent devotion to duty, regardless of personal inconvenience; a loyal man is prepared to make sacrifices for the sake of his allegiance to his sovereign, his country, his duty. A diplomat, like any other man, is governed by several loyalties. His success lies in his ability to strike a balance between his different loyalties which at times appear to be conflicting. The phenomenon of a diplomat falling in love with the country of his accreditation is all too common. Though springing from the sincerest of motives, such love may stand in the way of loyalty. To a diplomat who loves the country to which he is accredited, the vices and weaknesses of that country and its people cease to exist, for he sees nothing but good. And if he happens to dislike a country or its people he tends to become oblivious of its virtues and sees nothing but its vices. In both cases he allows his loyalty to be blurred, he loses his sense of perspective, and his value as a diplomat diminishes in proportion to the strength of his likes and dislikes.

In Communist and totalitarian countries loyalty is identified with a blind faith in the infallibility and justice of the prevailing regime. Hitler is known to have valued a soldier's blind faith in the final victory of the German army far more than any degree of professional integrity, and he is known to have ordered the dismissal of officers who reported objectively on an unfavourable situation. Communist diplomats are trained to disbelieve factual evidence if it does not fit in with their preconceived ideas and contradicts their doctrine. When facts are too obvious to be ignored they are forced to misinterpret them in order to refute any suggestion that they have been contaminated by other ideologies. In the Western world today, especially in the U.S.A., one can notice a growing tendency to identify the loyalty of civil servants, including diplomats, with sympathy for the government's policy and a prior acceptance of any conclusions which may flow from these policies. By putting the cart before the horse such a government deliberately denies itself the benefits of a foreign service and exposes itself to all the degrees of ignorance.

A diplomat is not always conscious of being disloyal when he proceeds with a 'civil leer' to execute a directive he does not endorse. Nor is he aware of having lost his loyalty when he allows personal rivalries and friction with his headquarters to affect both his outlook and his output. Many a silent act of disloyalty is committed because the man guilty of such breaches is not always loyal to himself. In disregard of the dictates of his duty, he does not hesitate to dictate dispatches with an eye on the fact that they should not prove distasteful to his superiors at home. In an effort to win their favour he indulges in exaggerations or resorts to a simple suppression of facts. In either case his attitude is inconsistent with loyalty. All this happens because he fails to develop a clear concept of loyalty; he has no understanding of the relative importance of his various obligations (to government, state, or God) which he often confuses and sometimes neglects.

The Prophet was a supreme example of loyalty. In faithfully discharging all his manifold duties, he never lost sight for a moment of the goal towards which all his activities were concentrated. Any action, any movement, any event which helped him bring nearer the object was a step in the right direction even though it meant immediate suffering and sacrifice. Every action, every movement, every event which tended to take him away from the object was a step in the wrong direction even though it meant immediate success, wealth or renown. One need not consult a complex moral code to guide one's steps. If one is true to one's self, one will not be untrue to others. If one is loyal to one's self, one will not be disloyal to others. Loyalty, in the final analysis, is but a faithful allegiance to one's own higher self—a law not imposed from without, but one's own law, one's own command springing from within.

The Prophet owed but one loyalty—all other loyalties were subordinated to the overriding considerations of his loyalty to God. The Prophet served but one Master— and all others were subordinated to the demands of His Law. There was no room for confusion and there was no occasion for conflict. His was a life of perfect harmony and perfect dedication. There was no conflict of loyalties because there was only one loyalty; there was no confusion of allegiance because there was only one Master. And to this Master the Prophet surrendered all his activities and all his judgments with a perfect spontaneity which is as surprising for the world as it was simple for Muhammad.

> Whosoever surrendereth his purpose to Allah while doing good, his reward is with his Lord; and there shall no fear come upon them, neither shall they grieve.[58]

The Qur'an mentions two types of people. There is the type of man who is glib and worldly-wise, pleasant and eloquent, the mischief-maker with a smooth tongue who indulges in plausible talk and often succeeds in realising his fraud without the victim even understanding the import of his dazzling and disarming approach. The glib hypocrite who appears worldly-wise but plans harm is contrasted with the other type of man—sincere, firm, devoted, willing to give his life for the faith that is in him. Muslims are asked to follow this type of which the Prophet is indeed the best example. This type[59] of man was not uncommon in the early days of Islam.

Muhammad owed many loyalties. He owed loyalty to those who had brought him up when he was an orphan; he owed loyalty to those who had helped him when he was helpless; he owed loyalty to his close companions who placed themselves completely at his disposal; he owed an obligation to his wives and relatives; he owed a duty to the sick, the slave and the poor; he owed a duty to his children and the children of others who were orphans like himself; and he owed a loyalty to the mass of Muslims who gave him succour and strength. But with all his varied loyalties Muhammad did not allow any one of them to blur his sense of perspective and involve him in a conflict which might deflect him from the path of duty and truth and induce him to forget his highest loyalty. Undaunted by the uproar of the Ansar in the hour of his conquest in Mecca he stood by his loyalty to his cause even though it appeared, for a while, that it might cost him all his following. The devotion of his close companions did not deflect him from his duty, for he did not court their pleasure when he took a decision against their advice. The love of his relatives did not prevent him from performing his duty; and the love of riches did not draw him away from his stand. All his efforts, all his energy, all his plans and all his patience were directed to one goal, one aim and one object—the faithful performance of duty. Any loyalty which stood in the way of duty was discarded directly. So complete was his surrender to duty that the Prophet could declare:

Lo, my worship and my sacrifice, and my living and my dying are for Allah, Lord of the worlds, and I am first of those who surrender (unto Him).[60]

It is this spontaneous surrender, this harmony, this integration, this clarity, this moving conviction and unfaltering faith, which make it possible for the Prophet of Islam to set an example of the loftiest.

NOTES

Introduction to the First Edition

1. L. Oppenheim, *International Law*, Vol. I, p. 62.
2. Aristotle, *Politics*, Book I, Chapter 7.
3. For more details see C. Phillipson, *The International Law and Customs of Ancient Greece and Rome*, 2 volumes.
4. The Qur'an, xlix. 13.
5. Ibid., ii. 62.
6. *De Jure Belli ac Pacis*, published c.e. 1625.
7. M. Hamidullah, *Muslim Conduct of State*, Lahore, Shaikh Muhammad Ashraf, 1953, p. 65.
8. For some Persian sayings and examples of this nature, see *Kitab al-Taj* attributed to Jahiz, Chapter I, pp. 121–23.

Chapter 1
PRINCIPAL NEGOTIATIONS

1. B. 'Abdul Dar.
2. B. 'Adiy b. Ka'b Lu'ayy.
3. Abu Umayya b. al-Mughira b. 'Abdullah b. 'Umar b. Makhzum.
4. Shibli, the Indian biographer of the Prophet, places this incident in the twenty-fifth year of his life while Ibn Ishaq places it in the thirty-fifth. See *Sirat Rasul Allah* translated by Alfred Guillaume (*The Life of Muhammad*, London, Oxford University Press, 1955), p. 84. In subsequent notes this translation will be referred to as *Sirat*.
5. Hamza b. Abdul Muttalib, uncle of the Prophet.
6. *Sirat*, p. 132.
7. The Qur'an, xli. 5.
8. *Sirat*, p. 133.
9. The Qur'an, ix. 40.
10. Ibn Khaldun, *History*, p. 126.
11. Montgomery Watt, *Muhammad at Medina*, Oxford, Clarendon Press, 1956, pp. 221–25.
12. I have not entirely adopted Watt's translation of the text of the treaty. The battle took place in a.h. 2.

13. The battle took place in A.H. 3.

14. An influential Muslim from Medina who tried to wreck Islam from within.

15. It was in this battle that Wahshi, the Abyssinian who was later to come as an envoy of the Quraysh to the Prophet, barbarously murdered Hamza, the uncle of the Prophet. Hind, the wife of Abu Sufyan, tore out the liver from the body of Hamza and chewed it up.

16. The Qur'an, xlviii. 24.

17. 'Uthman became the third Caliph of Islam. He succeeded 'Umar b. al-Khattab.

18. بسم الله الرحمن الرحيم

19. باسمك اللهم

20. Almost every commentator of the Qur'an has yielded to the temptation of translating the word *Rahman* as the 'merciful' instead of treating it as a proper noun, which it is intended to be at all places of the Qur'an. Take for example Sura 'al-Rahman,' which deals with this particular objection of the Quraysh. Even there the word *Rahman* is translated by the commentators as an attribute of God and not as a proper noun to which the Quraysh took serious exception. It will be recalled that the Quraysh accused the Prophet of having learned the Qur'an from a God called Rahman. Their objection to Rahman was so serious that they apprehended that all their gods including Allah would be placated by this new god called Rahman, which had been invented, according to them, by the Prophet.

Let us briefly refer to the Qur'an to bring out this point a little more clearly. Every time the Prophet approaches the Quraysh in Mecca with a message from his God, he is treated with ridicule. 'Is this,' they say, 'the one who talks of our gods?' and instead of attacking the core of the message conveyed by the Prophet, it is the god Rahman who is particularly picked up for ridicule for the very mention of the word which to them represented an innovation and a departure from their tradition. 'Still they deny Rahman; say: He is my Lord, there is no god but He' (xiii. 30). In this verse, the Qur'an clearly states that the Quraysh denied the existence of Rahman, the very mention of which was anathema to them. This is the background to the early history of Islam in which this ideological conflict between the concept of Allah and the concept of Rahman played a significant part in the initial stages of the development of Islam. Our translators do not appear to be sufficiently conscious of this phase. *The Encyclopaedia of Islam* does not have an independent article on *Rahman,* and dismisses it as an attribute of God, in a paragraph in the article on 'Allah.' It makes a cryptic reference to 'al-Rahman' being used at one time as a proper name equivalent to Allah, and the Meccans regarded this as one of the Prophet's innovations.

The Encyclopaedia of Islam concludes its remarks with the sentence: 'Compare the story of the Treaty of Hudaybiya where they rejected the formula containing it (Rahman) and insisted on the old Meccan form "In thy name" (باسمك اللهم) .'

21. قالوا و ما الرحمن

22. The Qur'an, xvii. 110.

23. Sarakhsiy, Vol. IV, p. 61; Lammens, *La Mecque,* p. 136.

24. *Sirat,* p. 505.

25. The Qur'an, xlviii. 1.

26. *Sirat,* pp. 552–53.

27. She tore open the liver from the body of the Prophet's uncle in the battle of Uhud, outside Medina.

28. *Sirat,* p. 550.

29. Now a well some fourteen miles from Mecca. It is also one of the stations from which pilgrims wear their *ihram* for 'Umra.

30. *Sirat,* pp. 592–93.

31. Ibid, pp. 593–94.

32. A.H. 2.

33. *Sirat,* p. 492.

34. This account is based on *Sirat-i-'A'yesha,* a biography by Sayyid Sulayman Nadvi, pp. 73–85.

35. The Qur'an, xxiv. 11–20.

36. Ibid, xxiv. 22.

Chapter 2
DELEGATIONS RECEIVED AND DISPATCHED

1. For details see M. Hamidullah, op. cit., pp. 123–25.

2. al-Tabari, *History,* Vol. I, pp. 1801–2.

3. *Sirat,* p. 649.

4. For a detailed discussion on the position and privileges of envoys, see Sarakhsiy, Vol. IV, p. 320.

5. *Sirat,* p. 615.

6. al-Tabari, *History,* Vol. I, p. 1826.

7. *Fatawa-i-'Alamgiri,* Vol. III, pp. 265–66.

8. *Sirat,* pp. 271–73.

9. Ibid., pp. 276–77.

10. Ibid., p. 277.

11. Ibid.

12. Ibid., p. 635.

13. Ibid., pp. 637–39.

14. Ibid., p. 628.

15. Ibid., p. 629.

16. Ibid.

17. Ibid., pp. 630–31.

18. Ibid., pp. 636–37.

19. Ibid., p. 649.

20. Ibid.

21. The Himyarites came to power in about 115 B.C. During this period the Romans attempted an invasion of Arabia. The expedition under Aelium Gallus (24 B.C.), however, came to grief, as it was lost in the desert on account of the refusal of the guides to cooperate in subjugating their brethren in Arabia. The Himyarite kings were overthrown by the Abyssinians in the fourth century C.E. Some of them accepted Judaism and founded a Jewish kingdom. The struggle between the Himyarites and the Abyssinians, therefore, assumed a new significance in that it became a struggle between Judaism and Christianity. It was perhaps on this account that Christian Abyssinia was

supported by Byzantium in its attempts to regain power. The Abyssinians succeeded in C.E. 525, but fifty years later the Persians, who had been called in by the opponents of Christianity, succeeded in taking over the rule.

22. *Sirat*, pp. 643–44.
23. In the last decade of the fifth century a new power arose in Central Arabia. The tribe of Kinda under the sway of the family of Akil al-Murar, who came from the South, stood in much the same relation to the rulers of the Yemen as the people of Hira to the Persians and the Ghassanids to Rome. Abraha in his invasion of the Hijaz was accompanied by chiefs of Kinda. Details of their history are not known, but they seem to have gained power at one time even over the Lakhmids of Hira and to have ruled over Bahrayn as well as Yamamah until the battle of Shi'b al-Jabala, when they lost this province of Hira. The poet Imru' al-Qays was a member of the princely family of Kinda.
24. *Sirat*, pp. 151–52.
25. Ibid., p. 657.
26. Ibid., pp. 647–48.
27. Ibid., p. 655.
28. Ibid., p. 656.
29. Ibid., pp. 656–57.

Chapter 3
THE MORAL DIPLOMACY

1. The Qur'an, iii. 134.
2. Ibid, xlii. 37.
3. Ibid., vii. 199.
4. Ibid., vi. 68.
5. Ibid., xvi. 125–28.
6. Ibid., iii. 159.
7. Ibid., xxiv. 62–63.
8. Ibid., xvii. 53–55.
9. Ibid., ii. 104.
10. Ibid., xlii. 15.
11. Ibid., xiv. 24–25.
12. Ibid., ii. 10.
13. Ibid., iii. 159.
14. Ibid., xxx. 19.
15. Ibid., ix. 97.
16. Ibid., xx. 43–44.
17. Ibid., xx. 49.
18. Ibid., xx. 50.
19. Ibid., xx. 51.
20. Ibid., xx. 52.
21. Ibid., lii. 48.
22. Ibid., lxxxii. 21–22.
23. Ibid., iii. 158.
24. Ibid., xxxiii. 72.
25. Ibid., xxiii. 8.

26. Ibid., ii. 83.
27. Ibid., xvii. 34.
28. Ibid., xiii. 20.
29. Ibid., v. 1.
30. A. Yusuf Ali, *The Holy Qur'an*, text, translation and commentary, Lahore, Shaikh Muhammad Ashraf, n.d., p. 238, note 682.
31. The Qur'an, xvi. 91.
32. Ibid., xvi. 92.
33. Ibid., ix. 1–2.
34. Sarakhsiy, Vol. IV, p. 7.
35. The Qur'an, ix. 4.
36. Ibid., ix. 7.
37. Ibid., xxii. 96.
38. On the manner of negotiation with princes; on the uses of diplomacy; the choice of ministers and envoys; and the personal qualities necessary for success in missions abroad.
39. The Qur'an, xiv. 24–26.
40. Ibid.
41. Ibid, xv. 94.
42. Ibid., xvi. 214.
43. Ibid., lxxx. 1–12.
44. Ibid., viii. 67–68.
45. Ibid., ix. 92.
46. Ibid., ix. 43.
47. Ibid., ii. 79.
48. Ibid., ii. 174.
49. Ibid., lii. 48.
50. Ibid., xxx. 60.
51. Ibid., xlvi. 35.
52. Not named in the Qur'an, but believed to be Khidr-Elias.
53. The Qur'an, ii. 108.
54. Ibid., xxxi. 18.
55. Ibid., vii. 37.
56. Ibid., vii. 188.
57. *Mohamed und Sein Werk*, p. 267.
58. The Qur'an, ii. 112.
59. Ibid., ii. 204–8.
60. Ibid., vi. 163.

SELECT BIBLIOGRAPHY

Ameer Ali, Syed. *Spirit of Islam*. London: Christopher, 1923.

Azad, Maulana Abu'l-Kalam. *Tarjuman al-Qur'an*. Vol. 1. Karachi: Maktaba-i-Sa'id. Vol. 2. Lahore: Maktaba-i-Mustafa'i.

Baker, Ernest. *The Politics of Aristotle*. London: Oxford University Press, 1946.

de Callieres, François. *On the Manner of Negotiating with Princes*. Translated by A. F. Whyte. Boston: Houghton, Mifflin & Co., 1919.

Encyclopaedia of Islam. London: Luzac & Co., 1913.

Fatawa-i-'Alamgiri.

Grotius, Hugo. *De Jure Belli ac Pacis*.

Hamidullah, Muhammad. *Muslim Conduct of State*. Lahore: Shaikh Muhammad Ashraf, 1953.

Ibn Ishaq. *Sirat Rasul Allah*. Translated by Alfred Guillaume. London: Oxford University Press, 1955.

Ibn Khaldun. *Kitab al-'Ibar*. ("History.") Cairo, 1957.

———. *Muqaddima*. ("*Prolegomena*.") Beirut, 1900.

al-Jahiz, *al-Bayan wa'l Tabyin*. Cairo: Matba'at al-Futuh al-Adabīya, 1902.

Muir, William. *The Life of Mahomet*. Edinburgh: Edinburgh University Press, 1912.

Nadvi, Sayyid Sulayman. *Sirat-i-'A'yesha*. A'zamgarh, India: Ma'araf Press.

Oppenheim, Lassa. *International Law*. London: Longmans, Green & Co., 1952.

Phillipson, Coleman. *The International Law and Customs of Ancient Greece and Rome.* 2 vols. London: Macmillan, 1915.

Pickthall, Mohammed Marmaduke. *The Meaning of the Glorious Koran.* London: G. Allen & Unwin, 1930.

al-Sarakhsi, Shams al-Din. *Kitab al-Mabsut.* 30 vols.

Shibli-Nu'mani, Maulana, *Sirat-al-Nabi.* 6 vols. A'zamgarh, India: Ma'araf Press.

al-Tabari. *Tarikh al-Rusul wa'l-Muluk.* ("History.") Cairo: al-Matba'at al-Muniriya, 1939.

Watt, Montgomery. *Muhammad at Medina.* Oxford: Clarendon Press, 1956.

Yusuf Ali, Abdullah. *The Holy Quran.* Text, translation and commentary. Lahore: Shaikh Muhammad Ashraf, n.d.

INDEX

★ OF RELATED INTEREST ★

THE CUP OF JAMSHID:
A Collection of Original Ghazal Poetry Translated from the
Urdu by the Author. Contains "An Introduction to Ghazal,"
Notes and Glossary.
BY MUHAMMAD DAUD RAHBAR
ISBN: 0–89007–001–4

★ Additional titles from "THE GOD SERIES" ★

SPIRITUAL PRACTICES:
Memorial Edition with Reminiscences by His Friends
BY SWAMI AKHILANANDA
ISBN: 0–89007–001–6

GOD OF ALL:
Sri Ramakrishna's Approach to Religious Plurality.
BY CLAUDE ALAN STARK
ISBN: 0–89007–000–8

GOD IN AFRICA:
Conceptions of God in African Traditional Religion
& Christianity
BY MALCOLM J. McVEIGH
ISBN: 0–89007–003–2

GOD AS MOTHER:
A Feminine Theology in India.
BY CHEEVER MACKENZIE BROWN
FOREWORD BY DANIEL H. H. INGALLS
ISBN: 0–89007–004–0

BEAUTY UNKNOWN:
Twenty-Seven Psychic Drawings of Spirit Beings with Their
Messages for Our Planet.
THROUGH DAPHNE & NELSON
ISBN: 0–89007–007–5

Claude Stark & Co.
PUBLISHERS, BOX 431, WEST DENNIS
CAPE COD, MASSACHUSETTS 02670, U.S.A.

order form

THE GOD SERIES:

Approaches to the Direct Experience of God

I wish to order the following clothbound books in the quantities indicated:

Quantity Amount

THE CUP OF JAMSHID by Muhammad Daud Rahbar (#900) @ $7.00 per copy   _____ $_____

SPIRITUAL PRACTICES by Swami Akhilananda (#100) @ $8.50 per copy   _____ _____

GOD OF ALL by Claude Alan Stark (#101) @ $12.00 per copy   _____ _____

GOD IN AFRICA by Malcolm J. McVeigh (#200) @ $8.00 per copy   _____ _____

GOD AS MOTHER by Cheever Mackenzie Brown (#106) @ $15.00 per copy   _____ _____

BEAUTY UNKNOWN through Daphne & Nelson (#500) @ $7.00 per copy   _____ _____

GOD SERIES: COMPLETE SET OF SIX BOOKS, save $7.50 (#190) @ $50.00 per set   _____ _____

Thank you for your order.   TOTAL $_____

☐ Send me your current catalog and place my name on your mailing list.

OVER FOR NAMES & ADDRESSES

THE GOD SERIES from *Claude Stark & Co.*

Please send me the books indicated on side 1, postpaid:

ORDERED BY _____ Date ____ , __ /19 ‘

_____ Zip _____

Enclosed is my check or money order in U.S. funds for $ _____ to Claude Stark & Co.

I understand my order will be shipped promptly.

Send the following book(s) as gifts: Send these book(s) as gifts too:

_____   _____

_____   _____

_____   _____

Ship to _____   Ship to _____

_____ Zip _____   _____ Zip _____

Please sign card   Please sign card

ORDER DEPARTMENT

Claude Stark & Co.
PUBLISHERS, Box 431, West Dennis
Cape Cod, Massachusetts 02670, U.S.A.